England's Most Famous Palaces: The History of Buckingham Palace and Kensington Palace

By Charles River Editors

D. Illif's picture of Buckingham Palace

About Charles River Editors

Charles River Editors is a boutique digital publishing company, specializing in bringing history back to life with educational and engaging books on a wide range of topics. Keep up to date with our new and free offerings with this 5 second sign up on our weekly mailing list, and visit Our Kindle Author Page to see other recently published Kindle titles.

We make these books for you and always want to know our readers' opinions, so we encourage you to leave reviews and look forward to publishing new and exciting titles each week.

Introduction

Buckingham Palace

"We think of medieval England as being a place of unbelievable cruelty and darkness and superstition. We think of it as all being about fair maidens in castles, and witch-burning, and a belief that the world was flat. Yet all these things are wrong." - Terry Jones

"I'm glad we've been bombed. It makes me feel I can look the East End in the face." - The Queen Mother in 1940 after Buckingham Palace had been bombed by the Nazis

When people think of the British Royal family, and more specifically where they live, the first image that often pops into mind is that of stately Buckingham Palace, with its changing of the guard and the occasional royal coach leaving or entering. Others may think of the royal country estate of Windsor Castle, a favorite of both Britain's longest-reigning and second longest-reigning monarchs. And there was a time when both royal residences played second fiddle to a much better known home, the elegant Kensington Palace.

In his multi-volume work, *Old and New London* (1878), Edward Walford wrote, "It has often been said by foreigners that if they were to judge of the dignity and greatness of a country by the palace which its sovereign inhabits, they would not be able to ascribe to Her Majesty Queen Victoria that proud position among the 'crowned heads' of Europe which undoubtedly belongs to her. But though Buckingham Palace is far from being so magnificent as Versailles is, or the Tuilleries once were, yet it has about it an air of solidity and modest grandeur, which renders it no unworthy residence for a sovereign who cares more for a comfortable home than for display."

This is ultimately what palaces are all about: power and impressions. Buckingham Palace is not different, for though it was originally built as a home of a private citizen, once a king bought it, its future was sealed. Walford continued, "Indeed, it has often been said that, with the exception of St. James's, Buckingham Palace is the ugliest royal residence in Europe; and although vast sums of money have been spent at various times upon its improvement and embellishment, it is very far from being worthy of the purpose to which it is dedicated—lodging the sovereign of the most powerful monarchy in the world. It fronts the western end of St. James's Park, which here converges to a narrow point; the Mall, upon the north, and Birdcage Walk, upon the south, almost meeting before its gates."

Kensington Palace

Steve Cadman's picture of the south front of Kensington Palace

"We think of medieval England as being a place of unbelievable cruelty and darkness and superstition. We think of it as all being about fair maidens in castles, and witch-burning, and a belief that the world was flat. Yet all these things are wrong." - Terry Jones

When people think of the British Royal family, and more specifically where they live, the first image that often pops into mind is that of stately Buckingham Palace, with its changing of the guard and the occasional royal coach leaving or entering. Others may think of the royal country estate of Windsor Castle, a favorite of both Britain's longest-reigning and second longest-reigning monarchs. But there was a time when both royal residences played second fiddle to a much better known home, the elegant Kensington Palace.

Like many royal residences, Buckingham and Kensington began their lives as large private homes, and it was only after a king, or in Kensington's case, a king and queen, took notice of them that they were expanded into the size and grandeur that they display today. Even this work was not the product of one major overhaul but of several, spread across decades of changes in architecture, interior design, and even technology.

King William III purchased Kensington Palace in the early years of his reign, less than three short decades after the Stuarts returned to the throne, and he and his queen were the first monarchs to move the British court there. Later, his successors became more attached to the palace, and by the time King George I, the first king from the House of Hanover, came to the throne, Kensington was considered the best place for the king and his family to live.

Ultimately, this did not last for long, because in spite of all the work King George I and King George II put into the palace, King George III preferred to live elsewhere, primarily the new Buckingham House. As a result, Kensington became the home of lesser royals, such as the penniless Duchess of Kent, who raised her little daughter, Victoria, there. Later one of England's most famous queens, this little girl grew up to use Kensington as a place to house relatives that she wanted to keep close by or felt some other moral obligation to.

In the century that followed Queen Victoria's reign, the palace became something of a "starter home" for newlywed princes and princesses, from the star-crossed Charles and Diana to the ever-popular Will and Kate. In fact, it is quite likely that young Prince George or his sister, Princess Charlotte, may one day begin their married lives in the house.

Even as Kensington Palace continues to have a formal role, it is far more than a royal residence today. For more than a century, many of the State Rooms formerly used to house monarchs have served as a popular museum for both those from London and the millions of tourists that visit the city each year. These rooms, along with the famous Kensington Gardens, have become one of the most popular sites in the nation, and are likely to remain so for years to come.

England's Most Famous Palaces: The History of Buckingham Palace and Kensington Palace

examines the long and storied history of two of England's most famous landmarks. Along with pictures depicting important people, places, and events, you will learn about Buckingham Palace and Kensington Palace like never before.

Buckingham Palace

Mulberry Garden and Arlington House

Ironically, Buckingham Palace's original site rails against the idea of formality. England's most well-known palace is located on a piece of land known colloquially as the Mulberry Garden, located in one of the most fashionable resorts in London and named for the trees that had been planted there by King James I. The king hoped England could use the trees to feed silk worms that could in turn make the nation less dependent on Chinese imports.

King James I of England

Ultimately, the plan proved to be a failure because the cold, wet English climate was inhospitable to silkworms, so the king graciously turned the Garden over to his people to use as a public park. However, unrest would come to England about a generation later, and on May 10, 1654, diarist John Evelyn hinted at it when he complained, "My Lady Gerrard treated us at

Mulberry Gardens, now the only place of refreshment about the Town for persons of the best quality to be exceedingly cheated at: Cromwell and his partisans having shut up and closed Spring Gardens which until now had been the usual rendezvous for the Ladies and Gallants of this season." One of Evelyn's contemporaries, Samuel Pepys, called it "a silly place, with a wilderness somewhat pretty," and Clement Walker, author of *Anarchia Anglicana* (1649), suggested it was a seedy place while writing about "new-erected sodoms and spintries at the Mulberry Garden at S. James's..."

Pepys

With these and other similar complaints in mind, King Charles II decided to close the park and give the land instead to the Earl of Arlington, Henry Bennet. Historian Thomas Babington Macaulay observed that Bennet "had some talent for conversation and some for transacting ordinary business of office. He had learned during a life passed in travel and negotiating, the art of accommodating his language and deportment to the society in which he found himself. His vivacity in the closet amused the King; his gravity in debates and conferences imposed on the public, and he had succeeded in attaching to himself, partly by services, partly by hopes a considerable number of personal retainers." Likewise, the Comte de Gramont claimed that the Earl of Arlington had mastered "the gravity and solemn mien of the Spaniards, a scar across the bridge of his nose, which he covered with a little lozenge shaped plaster, gave a secretive and mysterious air to his visage [with] an overwhelming anxiety to thrust himself forward which passed for industry … and an impenetrable stupidity which passed for the power to keep a secret."

Charles II

Bennet

In his "Art of Cookery," Dr. William King observed in 1708,

> "The fate of things lies always in the dark:
> What cavalier would know St. James's Park?
> For 'Locket's' stands where gardens once did spring,
> And wild ducks quack where grasshoppers did sing:
> A princely palace on that space does rise,
> Where Sedley's noble muse found mulberries."

Arlington House seemed destined for fame from the beginning; in fact, it was here that the first cup of English tea was served. However, the house had only a short life, and in short order the house was torn down and the land on which it sat was sold to John Sheffield, the Duke of Buckingham, who built his home out more durable red brick. According to Macauley, the Duke had tried his hand at a seafaring career and like, "any lad of noble birth, any dissolute courtier, for whom one of the king's mistresses would speak a word, might hope [for] a ship of the line … If in the interval of feasting, drinking and gambling, he succeeded in learning the names of the points of the compass, he was thought fully qualified to take charge of a three decker…In 1666, John Sheffield, Earl of Mulgrave, at seventeen years of age, volunteered to serve at sea against the Dutch. He passed six weeks on board, diverting himself [with] young libertines of rank and then returned home to take command of a troop of horse. After this he was never on the water till the year 1672 when he was appointed Captain of a ship of 84 guns, reputed the finest in the navy. He was then 23 years old ... As soon as he came back from sea, he was made Colonel of a regiment of foot."

The Duke of Buckingham

Buckingham House

According to *New View of London*, (1708), Buckingham House was "a graceful palace, very commodiously situated at the westerly end of St. James's Park, having at one view a prospect of the Mall and other walks, and of the delightful and spacious canal; a seat not to be condemned by the greatest monarch...It consists of the mansion house, and at some distance from each end of that, conjoined by two arching galleries, are the lodging-rooms for servants on the south side of the court; and opposite, on the north side, are the kitchen and laundry, the fronts of which are elevated on pillars of the Tuscan, Doric, and Ionic orders, thereby constituting piazzas...The walls are brick; those of the mansion very fine rubbed and gagged, adorned with two ranges of pilasters of the Corinthian and Tuscan orders. On the latter (which are uppermost) is an acrogeria of figures, standing erect and fronting the court; they appear as big as life and look noble…The hall, partly paved with marble, is adorned with pilasters, the intercolumns are noble painture in great variety, and on a pedestal near the foot of the great staircase (whose steps are entire slabs) are the marble figures of Cain killing his brother Abel. In short, the whole structure is spacious, commodious, rich, and beautiful, but especially in the finishing and furniture. This house is now in the occupation of his Grace the Duke of Buckingham. It has a spacious court on its easterly side, fenced with a handsome wall, iron-work, and a beautiful iron gate, where the duke's coronet, arms, garter, and George are exquisitely represented in iron."

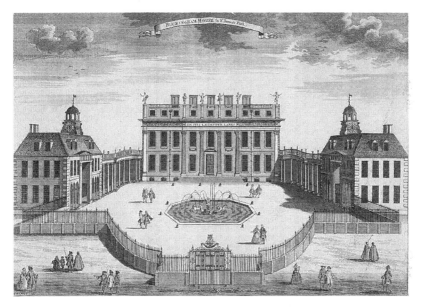

Buckingham House circa 1710

Writing toward the end of his life, the Duke himself described his residence: "I rise now in summer, about seven o'clock in a very large bedchamber (entirely quiet, high and free from the early sun) to walk in the garden or, if raining in a Salon filled with pictures, some good, but none disagreeable; There also, in a row above them, I have so many portraits of famous persons … as are enough to excite ambition in any man less lazy, or less at ease, than myself." He called his garden "the noblest that can be, presenting at once to view a vast Town, a Palace & a magnificent Cathedral…I confess myself so changed … as to my former enchanting delights, that the company I commonly find at home is agreeable enough to make me conclude the evening on a delightful Terrace. …though of more satisfaction to me than all the rest … and 'tis the little closet of books at the end of that green house which joins the best apartment, which besides their being so very near, are ranked in such a method, that by its mark a very Irish footman may fetch any book I want."

Unfortunately for Buckingham, his only legitimate son died unmarried without producing an heir, so the family lost its title in 1735. However, Buckingham's widow, Catherine Darnley, insisted on keeping the house. She was the illegitimate daughter of King James II, and historian J. H. Jesse noted one of her customs at the residence: "Here, on each successive anniversary of the execution of her grandfather, Charles I, she was accustomed to receive her company in the grand drawing-room, herself seated in a chair of state, clad in the deepest mourning, and surrounded by her women, all as black and as dismal looking as herself. Here, too, that eccentric lady breathed her last." In one of his famous letters, contemporary Horace Walpole wrote humorously, "Princess Buckingham, is either dead or dying. She sent for Mr. Anstes, and settled the ceremonial of her burial. On Saturday she was so ill that she feared dying before the pomp was come home. She said, 'Why don't they send the canopy for me to see? Let them send it, even though all the tassels are not finished.' But yesterday was the greatest stroke of all. She made her ladies vow to her that, if she should lie senseless, they would not sit down in the room before she was dead."

Fortunately, the old duke had another son, and though Charles Herbert Sheffield was born on the wrong side of the blanket, he nonetheless inherited the house after Darnley's death. He was more interested in money than his home, and in 1754 he tried to sell Buckingham House as a home for the newly established British Museum. He wrote to a trustee, "In pursuance to your commands I have considered what value to put upon my House, Gardens and Fields for which I hope if it should suit SR Hans Sloane's Trustees they won't think Thirty Thousand Pounds too much; it having cost the old Duke twice that Sum but Fifty years ago and Mr. Timbill, the Builder who was always reckoned an Honest able Man in his Profession valued it at more than [I ask] four years ago, since when I have layd out several Hundred Pounds in Repairing and Adorning it…"

Ultimately, they turned him down, so instead, Charles Herbert Sheffield sold it in 1761 to King George III for £21,000. That year, the Duke of Buckinghamshire wrote a letter to the Duke of Shrewsbury in which he described in detail the way that the exterior of Buckingham Palace looked at that time: "The avenues of this house, are along St. James's Park, through rows of good elms on one hand, and gay flourishing limes on the other; that for coaches, this for walking, with the Mall lying betwixt them. This reaches to an iron palisade that encompasses a square court, which has in the midst a great basin, with statues and water works, and from its entrance rises all the way imperceptibly, till we mount to a terrace in the front of a large ball, paved with square white stones, mixed with a dark colored marble…."

King George III

The duke also described the interior, writing that "on the right hand, we go into a parlour thirty-three feet by thirty-nine, with a niche fifteen feet broad for a beaufet, paved with white marble, and placed within an arch, with pilasters of divers colors, the upper part of which, as high as the ceiling, is painted by Ricci. From hence we pass through a suite of large rooms into a bedchamber of thirty-four feet by twenty-seven; within it a large closet that opens into a green-house…On the left hand of the hall are three stone arches, supported by three Corinthian pillars, under one of which we go up forty-eight steps, ten feet broad, each step of one entire Portland stone. These stairs, by the help of two resting places, are so very easy there is no need of leaning on the iron baluster…. the largeness of the whole had admitted of a sure remedy against any decay of the colors from saltpeter in the wall, by making another of oak laths four inches within it, and so primed over like a picture."

According to Buckinghamshire, the stairs ended on the second floor just outside double doors that opened into a large salon. There were a number of other rooms upstairs, several reached by what he called "great doors."

Fortunately for both the royal and common members of the household, the house was not designed simply to be beautiful but also to be functional. For one thing, the passages from the kitchen and to the cellars were covered so that the servants could carry out their work even in inclement weather. There were also two back staircases that allowed the servants to come and go upstairs without disturbing their masters, and without having to deal with running into them. The kitchen was also well designed for use and comfort, with 30 feet high ceilings and a cupola on top that dissipated the heat and odors that otherwise might have accumulated there. The larder and laundry were located near the kitchen.

On top of the palace roof was a lead cistern. A large pump kept this full of water from the Thames River, and according to Buckinghamshire, it held up to 12,500 gallons of water that was used for everything except drinking. Instead, the royals and their servants drank the beer brewed in the palace brew house, which was also located near the kitchen.

Once he purchased the property, the king naturally furnished it with the best items money could buy. To that end, he commissioned Vile & Cobb, master furniture makers. According to biographer J. T. Smith, Mr. Cobb was "a singularly haughty man, the upholsterer. One of the proudest men in England, he always appeared in full dress of the most superb and costly kind, whether strutting magnificently through his workshops, giving orders to his men, or on some errand at the 'Queen's House', where the King who smiled at his pomposity frequently employed him for cabinet work of an elaborate and expensive sort…His Majesty's library at the Queen's House when giving orders to a workman whose ladder chanced to stand before a book required by the King, His Majesty desired Cobb to hand him the work. Instead of obeying, Cobb called to his man, 'fellow, give me that book!' The King with his usual condescension rose and asked Cobb for his man's name. 'Jenkins, your Majesty,' answered the astonished upholsterer. 'Then,' observed the King, 'Jenkins. You shall hand me that book.'"

King George III also enjoyed purchasing fine furniture previously owned by others, as another writer reported: "On Monday his Majesty passed by West Thorpe House near Marlow, the seat of the late Governor Winch. He sent one of his Equerries to enquire whose goods were selling by auction; when Mr. Christie requested his most dutiful respects might be presented to his Majesty for he wished to show him some very curious ivory chairs and a couch that were to be disposed of." Could this be Mr. Christie of the soon to be famous auction house? The author continued, "His Majesty turned back, they were shown him on the lawn opposite the house and he liked them so well that he ordered them to be purchased for the Queen … the chairs cost 14½ guineas each, the couch 48 guineas and two small cabinets 45 guineas."

On March 23, 1767, Mrs. Philip Lybbe Powys described her visit to Buckingham: "The hall and staircase are particularly pleasing. The whole of the ground floor is for the King, whose apartments are fitted up rather neatly elegant than profusely ornamental. The library consists of three rooms, two oblong and one octagonal. The books are said to be the best collection anywhere to be met with…The Queen's apartments are ornamented as one expects a Queen's should be, with curiosities from every nation that can deserve her notice. The most capital pictures, the finest Dresden & other china, cabinets of more minute curiosities. Among the pictures let us note the famed cartoons from Hampton Court & a number of small & beautiful pictures; one room panelled with the finest Japan. The floors are all inlaid in the most expensive manner, and tho' but in March, every room was full of Roses, carnations, hyacinths etc, dispersed in the prettiest manner imaginable in jars & different flowerpots on stands. On her toilet, besides the gilt plate, innumerable knick-knacks…Round the dressing room, let into the crimson damask hangings in a manner uncommonly elegant, are frames of fine impressions, miniatures etc. It being at that time the coldest weather possible we were amazed to find so large a house so warm but fires, it seems, are kept the whole day, even in the closets, and to prevent accidents to furniture so costly from the neglect of the attendance, there is in every chimney a lacquered wire fire board, the cleverest contrivance that can be imagin'd as even the smallest spark cannot fly through them, while you have the heat & they are really ornamental."

In the years that followed, Buckingham House, as it was still known, was the site of more births than deaths. "Mad King George" and his wife had more than a dozen children, and as time passed, they became so enamored of the house that they decided to make it their permanent home, leaving St. James Palace to be used only for formal occasions of state. In 1775, Parliament formerly ceded Buckingham, not to George III, as might be assumed, but to his devoted wife, Queen Charlotte, in exchange for her giving up her home at Somerset House. Therefore, Buckingham House soon came to be known as the "Queen's House."

Queen Charlotte

Around the same time, in 1773, one Englishman described the house in less than glowing terms, writing, "In the front it is enclosed with a semi-circular sweep of iron rails, which are altered very unhappily from the rails which enclosed it before it became a royal residence. Formerly an elegant pair of gates opened in the middle; but now, though a foot-opening leads up to where an opening naturally is expected in front, all entrance is forbidden, by the rails being oddly continued across without affording an avenue through. Whoever seeks to enter must walk round either to the right or left, and in the corners perhaps he may gain admittance…The edifice is a mixture of brick and stone, with a broad flight of steps leading up to the door, which is between four tall Corinthian pilasters, which are fluted and reach up to the top of the second storey. … Behind the house is a garden and terrace, from which there is a fine prospect of the adjacent country."

About 25 years later, another author was more charitable, noting that Buckingham Palace "contains within apartments as spacious and commodious as any palace in Europe for state parade." Also, when the Prince of Wales, the future King George IV, married, "a suite of the principal rooms was fitted up in the most splendid manner; the walls of two of the levee rooms being hung with beautiful tapestry, then recently discovered with its colors unfaded in an old chest at St. James's…In the grand levee room, is a bed of crimson velvet, manufactured in Spitalfields. The canopy of the throne likewise is of crimson velvet, trimmed with broad gold lace, and embroidered with crowns set with fine pearls of great value. This was first used on Queen Charlotte's birthday, after the union of the kingdoms of Great Britain and Ireland, and the shamrock, the badge of the Irish nation, is interwoven with the other decorations of the crown with peculiar taste and propriety."

George IV

There was an unusual, octagonal apartment located in the southeast corner of the palace. Housed there was one of the premier collections of cartoons drawn by the famed Renaissance artist Raphael. There was also a throne room where Queen Charlotte received her most important visitors. However, for the most part, the future palace remained, as architect William Henry Leeds observed in 1838, "dull, dowdy, and decent; nothing more than a large, substantial, and respectable-looking red brick house; quite unsophisticated in its appearance, with the exception that it was garnished in the center with four Corinthian stone pilasters in a taste partaking more of the Dutch than the classical style…never the less such intermixture of brick and stone has been regarded rather as a beauty than otherwise by one critic, M. Quatremere de Roissy, who gives it as his opinion that red brick serving as a ground to columns and entablatures, sets them off to greater advantage. Most certainly such contrast of color and material does render the stone dressings more conspicuous, and where it is in unison with the style employed, such intermixture of material may be resorted to with advantage: but wherever orders — either Greek or Italian are employed, the effect is apt to be harsh and crude, as well as to partake of meanness."

No matter how the palace looked architecturally, it was still the home of the sovereigns, which ensured that it continued to attract the most prominent Englishmen, including those who enjoyed creating things of beauty. For instance, one artist wrote to a friend in 1770, "Last Monday, Mr. Wedgwood and I had a long audience of their Majesties, at the Queen's palace, to present some bas-reliefs which the Queen had ordered, and to show some new improvements, with which they were well pleased. They expressed in the most obliging and condescending manner their attention to our manufacture, and entered very freely into conversation on the further improvements of it, and on many other subjects." Of course, this was Wedgwood of china fame.

In 1779, a serious storm blew through London and seriously damaged Buckingham House. Mrs. Papendiek, whose father was a page at court, later recalled, "It took off the upper corner of the Queen's House. This was the room next to the one in which the Princes Ernest, Augustus & Adolphus slept, which was over the bedroom of their majesties. The King was up, and with his children in a moment. The ceiling was falling fast & had already already broken the bedstead of the elder Prince … but no harm happened to them." This incident forced the already busy king to pay more attention to his home, a problem he did not need in the middle of the American Revolution.

In addition to the trouble across the Atlantic, the late 18th century was a turbulent time in Europe, especially in England, where King George III was trying to fight wars on multiple fronts. In 1780, when riots broke out in London, George was forced to use Buckingham House as a fortress, clearly something it was never intended to be. He established the Queen's Riding House as a sort of command center, and one contemporary reported, "Between three and four thousand troops were in the Queen's Gardens, and surrounded Buckingham House. During the first night the alarm was so sudden, that no straw could be got for the troops to rest themselves on; which being told his Majesty, he, accompanied with one or two officers, went throughout the ranks…" According to the writer, the king said, "My lads, my crown cannot purchase you straw to-night; but depend on it, I have given orders that a sufficiency shall be here to-morrow forenoon; as a substitute for the straw, my servants will instantly serve you with a good allowance of wine and spirits, to make your situation as comfortable as possible; and I shall keep you company myself till morning." The report went on to say, "The King did so, walking mostly in the garden, sometimes visiting the Queen and the children in the palace, and receiving all messages in the Riding House, it being in a manner head-quarters. When he was told that part of the mob was attempting to get into St. James's Palace, he forbade the soldiers to fire, but ordered them to keep off the rioters with their bayonets."

Such actions made King George III popular with the common people, and his parties made him popular with his courtiers. In 1786, Sophie von la Roche recounted her visit to Buckingham House: "The noble simplicity of the furnishings, the order and neatness, were marks of the character of the owner – marks of the wise humility upon the throne. The library occupies the largest apartment and embraces the entire treasure-house of human knowledge. Three rooms are given up to it…Fine pictures by Van Dyck, a large number by Claude Lorrain, Guido Reni, Del Sarto, masterpieces by Angelica [Kauffmann] and some excellent miniatures render these simple damask hangings very valuable. In a small cabinet off the bedroom are the portraits of the fourteen royal children – thus the first waking moments are dedicated to this sight and the emotions of true motherhood…The concert hall contains a large organ…because the royal family holds private prayers to an organ accompaniment; for it has always been mainly associated with church music. The audience chamber is devoid of all splendour: one cabinet, however, is enhanced by the queen's tapestry-work. In a side room looking on to the garden an artist was at work; and there, too, we found two lovely portraits of the youngest princesses…There is a colonnade in the vestibule worthy of the dignity of this small palace's mistress…since the stairs are also decorated with frescoes … The choice of site for this palace is perfect, as it takes in the gradual incline, from which the royal park of St James's and Green Park can be completely overlooked, and at the back of it a pleasant garden has been laid out in which to take a solitary stroll."

She concluded by quoting Mr. Vulliamy, who said, "The eye of the queen spreads this elegance in Buckingham's house, just as her heart allows the king to savour the sweet happiness of purest love."

The 19th Century

Unfortunately, the entertainments held there were often far more elegant than their surroundings, for in the early years of the 19th century, as King George III began his descent into madness, Buckingham House once again fell into disrepair. In 1802, a reporter from the *Gentleman's Magazine* observed that the floors were "cold and hardrubbed…without a carpet, a luxury of which his majesty denies himself in almost every room." Attempting to improve her surroundings, one of the many princesses living in the household had painted (or perhaps more accurately, dyed) the velvet curtains "in shades of brown and maroon." However, the furniture remained "very plain and old fashion," made of materials that were "not always so … good, seldom so beautiful as would be required in the houses of many opulent individuals. Though old, the furniture bears no stamp of venerable antiquity. The damask of the curtains and chairs is much faded: the mahogany … is not beautiful: it is even so dull that it much resembles walnut; and the latter are made with curving legs, and clump or rather knob feet, not well carved."

In 1811, a Scottish artist, Charles Kirkpatrick Sharpe, complained to Lady Charlotte Campbell, "I was one of the happy few at H 's ball given in B--m House — a house I had been long anxious to see, as it is rendered classical by the pen of Pope and the pencil of Hogarth. It is in a woeful condition, and, as I hear, to be pulled down. The company was very genteel (I can't get a less vulgar word to express the sort of things) and very dull; but all the ladies were vastly refreshed with an inscription chalked upon the floor, which each applied to herself. Within a wreath of laurel, like burdock, fastened with fifty crooked true-love knots, were the mysterious words 'Pour elle.'"

Sharpe

In the 19th century, as in the 21st century, Buckingham Palace was used to impress upon visitors the importance and grandeur of the English monarchy. For instance, in 1809, when the Ambassador from Persia visited, the English were more than a little anxious to make a good impression, being still unfamiliar with the ways of the Far East. Thus, according to the records, when he arrived, "the great iron gates fronting the park were thrown open for his entrance."

One of the most long-lasting changes brought to English society began with Queen Charlotte, who wanted her children to enjoy the types of Christmas decorations she had had in her youth in Germany. Among these was a Christmas tree, an innovation among the British, who had never before had such an item. One courtier remembered, "It was hung with presents for the children, who were invited to see it; and I well remember the pleasure that it was to hunt for one's own name, which was sure to be attached to one or more of the pretty gifts."

By this time, much about the palace had changed, and the fourth volume of "The Ladies Cabinet of Fashion, Music and Nature" noted the changes made since Buckinghamshire's time: "The 'goodly elms and gay flourishing limes' went to decay. The 'iron palisade' assumed a more modern form; and of the 'great basin with statues and waterworks' no traces were left. Many of these statues were deposited in the famous lead statue yard, in Piccadilly; but that also in its turn ceased to exist; what became of the images we have not learnt. The terrace mentioned by the Duke was entirely done away, and the entrance came to be those small steps into the hall…The 'covered passage from the kitchen' was built up; the 'corridors supported on Ionic pillars' were filled in with brick work. and more modern door-ways, windows with compartments over them, inserted therein, with strings. plinth, &c., constituting concealed passages from the wings to the house. The Duke's 'kitchen, with an open cupola at top,' was at length nowhere to be found. The renovated plan, as seen externally, continued to be nearly the same, with the exception of the palisade, great basin, covered passages, the building up of the corridors, terrace, or flight of steps, and an additional door-way to the left wing…Festoons of flowers and fruit, which were under the windows of the principal floor, were cut out, and in their place the side balustrades remained in continuation. Sills of three mouldings only remained under the windows of the principal floor; a continued string occupied their place to the hall story; to the attic floor, architraves to the four sides of the windows of the wings common cills were given, &c. &c."

George III died in 1820 and was succeeded by his son, George IV. A few years into his reign, the new king, who loved to live lavishly, set about expanding the palace and making major renovations to both the interior and exterior of the building. The king chose John Nash, then the Official Architect to the Office of Woods and Forests, to head the work. Nash later wrote, "His late Majesty's intentions and commands were to convert Buckingham House into a private residence for himself. A plan was made upon a small scale, merely adding a few rooms to the old house. Whilst this plan was forming, and on my observing that the plan was being enlarged, I continually urged his Majesty to build in some other situation, and made several plans for that purpose, using all the arguments in my power to dissuade his Majesty from adding to the old Palace, but without any effect; for the late King constantly persisted that he would not build a new Palace, but would add to the present house."

Undeterred, he continued, "I then urged his Majesty to pull down the house, and rebuild it higher up in the garden in a line with Pall Mall. To induce his Majesty's acquiescence, I stated the lowness of the present site and the northern aspect, and recommended that the house should be placed on a level with Hyde Park Corner, and in a line with Pall Mall, a road or prolongation of which should cross the Green Park as an approach. This proposition I thought had some weight, and for a time I had hopes my recommendation would be adopted…."

He soon learned that the king would not be so easily swayed, especially when the sovereign said to another high ranking official in his presence, "Long, now remember I tell Nash before you at his peril, ever to advise me to build a palace. I am too old to build a palace, I have no objection to build one, but I must have a pied à terre. I do not like Carlton House standing in a street; and, moreover, I tell him I will have it at Buckingham House; and if he pulls it down he shall rebuild it in the same place; there are early associations which endear me to the spot."

Nash finally acquiesced. According to the Royal Trust, which today supervises the maintenance of Buckingham Palace, "During the last five years of George IV's life, Nash enlarged Buckingham House into the imposing U-shaped building which was to become Buckingham Palace. ... He extended the central block of the building westwards and to the north and south, and the two wings to the east were entirely rebuilt. The wings enclosed a grand forecourt which transformed the aspect of the Palace from St James's Park…Nash also created a triumphal arch in the center of the forecourt. The arch formed part of a ceremonial processional approach to the Palace and celebrated Britain's recent naval and military victories."

Nash

During this period, a popular ditty rose up concerning the newly improved palace. It went, in part:

> This is the Entrance, the Triumphal Arch,
>
> Which, 'tis said, will be probably finish'd in March,
>
> (And, compared with the elegant gates of Hyde Park,
>
> May justly be term'd tasteless, gloomy, and dark,)
>
> Which leads to the large Pond of Water, or Basin,
>
> Where the Royal Narcissus may see his dear face in,

Ere he rove 'mong the Pyramids, Temples, and Ditches,

Where Naiads and Cupids are seen without breeches,

(For such things in the West are allow'd, and thought pretty.

Though Venus and Cupids daren't go in the City,)

Who preside o'er the Fountains, the Promenades, and Rides,

(And 'twould puzzle old Harry to tell what besides,)

Which lead from the Hill, the magnificent Mound,

Thrown up in the Garden, full half a mile round.

To protect from the breeze and to hide from the people

Thickly planted with trees, and as high as a steeple,

These much-talk'd-of wings which by estimate round

Are said to have cost forty-two thousand pound.

And which not quite according with Royalty's taste.

Are doom'd to come down and be laid into waste;

(So to make up the loss of such changing and chopping,

The pay of poor clerks they're eternally docking,)

But they touch not the beautiful Ball in the Cup,

Which the tasteful Committee in wisdom set up

On the top of the Palace that N--H built.

The people's complaints were understandable, as the Royal Trust explained: "The Buckingham Palace created by Nash was widely regarded as a masterpiece. It came, however, at a considerable cost. By 1828 Nash had spent £496,169 on the changes to the building. Soon after the death of George IV two years later, the Prime Minister…dismissed Nash from his post for over-spending. Lord Duncannon, First Commissioner of Works, took over the task of overseeing the completion of the Palace. Duncannon appointed a new architect in Edward Blore, who extended the east façade at both ends and created a new entrance (the Ambassadors' Entrance) on the southern side. …the State Rooms were completed between 1833 and 1834."

An engraving depicting Buckingham Palace in the 1830s

As it turned out, King William IV, who succeeded his brother as king in 1830, had no desire to live in the palace and instead remained where he was in Clarence House. In fact, when fire severely damaged the Houses of Parliament in 1834, he offered Buckingham Palace as a replacement, assuring Parliament that he had no need for it. Parliament's leaders decided against taking over the former home of royalty and instead authorized sufficient funding to have the building properly completed for a royal home. This move proved very providential, because the string of old kings was about to give way to a young queen who would make her home there for much of the 19th Century.

King William IV

It is unlikely that anybody ever moved into Buckingham Palace with as much enthusiasm and joy as did the young Queen Victoria in 1837. She had grown up in Kensington Palace, which was by no means dreary, but her life there was, as she lived under the constant scrutiny of her mother and her mother's unscrupulous advisor, John Conroy. Victoria later recalled, "My earliest recollections are connected with Kensington Palace, where I can remember crawling on a yellow carpet spread out for that purpose -- and being told that if I cried and was naughty my 'Uncle Sussex' would hear me and punish me, for which reason I always screamed when I saw him! ... I used to ride a donkey given me by my Uncle, the Duke of York, who was very kind to me. ... To Tunbridge Wells we also went, living at a house called Mt. Pleasant, now an Hotel. Many pleasant days were spent here, and the return to Kensington in October or November was generally a day of tears."

Victoria as a teen

Victoria's mother, the Duchess of Kent

Biographer Kate Williams described these early years: "The duchess and Conroy attempted to bend Victoria to their will with a plan known as the 'Kensington system'. According to Victoria's half brother, Prince Charles of Leiningen, 'the basis of all actions, of the whole system followed at Kensington' was to ensure that the duchess had such influence over her daughter that 'the nation should have to assign her the regency', and the people would always associate her with Victoria. The aim was to make certain that 'nothing and no one should be able to tear the daughter away from her' … The Kensington system involved constant surveillance of the little girl 'down to the smallest and most insignificant detail'. Every cough, every piece of bread and butter consumed, every stamp of the tiny foot was reported to Conroy. The princess was forbidden the company of other children, and was never left alone. Although there were plenty of rooms, she slept in her mother's chamber and her governess sat with her until the duchess came to bed." In 1843, when she had been married for a few years to her beloved Albert and was herself a mother, Victoria admitted "that certainly my Kensington life for the last six or seven years had been one of great misery and oppression…"

Prince Albert

For the still young Victoria, Buckingham Palace symbolized freedom and a new life for herself, and what a life it was during those first carefree years of her reign, as she threw herself into enjoying all the pleasures that had been denied her as a girl. She had very little interest in the palace itself, other than as a backdrop for entertaining, and it was only later, after she married Prince Albert in 1840, that any real efforts were made to further improve the palace.

For all their great love for each other, Albert and Victoria were in many ways opposites. That extended to interior decorating; while she paid no attention to their home whatsoever, he was obsessed with every small detail of how the house operated. Accustomed as he was to German efficiency, he was appalled at the way the maintenance of his new home was handled. Under the supervision of Victoria's former governess, Baroness Louise Lehzen, the house was always dusty, and servants were allowed to do their jobs in a lax manner. In one of the most famous legends of the palace at that time, Albert asked his young wife why the windows were always dirty, and she replied airily that one team washed the insides while another washed the outsides and that they were never in sync.

Lehzen

Then there was the matter of security. In March 1841, a young man known as "the boy Jones" managed to break into the palace and roam the halls for some time before being caught. To make matters worse, this happened on more than one occasion. Writing in the *Journal*, a Mr. Raikes noted, "A little scamp of an apothecary's errand-boy, named Jones, has the unaccountable mania of sneaking privately into Buckingham Palace, where he is found secreted at night under a sofa, or some other hiding-place close to the Queen's bed-chamber. No one can divine his object, but twice he has been detected and conveyed to the police-office, and put into confinement for a time. The other day he was detected in a third attempt, with apparently as little object. Lady Sandwich wittily wrote that he must undoubtedly be a descendant of In-I-Go Jones, the architect."

In spite of these and other problems, Victoria's early years at Buckingham Palace were happy ones, and they set the tone for the future. Indeed, the elegant home became the backdrop for multiple births and marriages. In 1840, Victoria provided the country with an heir who bore her own name, and the following year, the infant Princess Victoria was supplanted in more ways than one by her brother, Bertie, who would become the future King Edward VII. To date, King Edward VII is the only monarch to both be born and die in Buckingham Palace, although it is possible in the future that he could be joined by his great-great-grandson, the current Prince Charles, who was also born there.

King Edward VII

In 1843, Victoria's cousin, Princess Augusta of Cambridge, married Frederick William, Grand Duke of Mecklenburg-Strelitz. Always anxious that her beloved husband should receive the respect he was due, and then some, she nearly made a scene at the wedding. Again, Raikes reported the story, told to him by the Duke of Wellington: "When we proceeded to the signatures of the bride and bridegroom, the King of Hanover was very anxious to sign before Prince Albert, and when the Queen approached the table, he placed himself by her side, watching his opportunity. She knew very well what he was about, and just as the Archbishop was giving her the pen, she suddenly dodged round the table, placed herself next to the Prince, then quickly took the pen from the Archbishop, signed, and gave it to Prince Albert, who also signed next, before it could be prevented."

The wedding may have been held in the new private chapel, completed that same year. The pious monarchs ordered it built in a comfortable space formerly occupied by a conservatory.

This was the first of a number of building projects commissioned in the years that followed, and by the time they were done, Victoria and her husband spent more than £150,000 renovating the east side of the building. The work took place under the watchful eye of architect Edward Blore, and so much was done that by 1851, Nash himself might not have recognized his own work. Most significantly, Blore moved Nash's famous Marble Arch from the palace's main entrance to the northeast corner of Hyde Park. While it had once displayed a banner indicating that the sovereign was in residence, that role was passed on to a flagpole sitting atop the palace itself.

Blore

In 1883, Noel Ruthven noted, "The new east front of the palace is the same length as the garden front; the height to top of the balustrade is nearly eighty feet, and it has a central and two arched side entrances, leading direct into the quadrangle. The wings are surmounted by statues representing 'Morning,' 'Noon,' and 'Night;' the 'Hours and the Seasons;' and upon turrets, flanking the central shield (bearing 'V. R. 1847'), are colossal figures of 'Britannia' and 'St. George;' besides groups of trophies, festoons of flowers, &c. Around the entire building is a scroll frieze of the rose, shamrock, and thistle."

Furthermore, he complained, "It has been asserted that the mismanagement on the part of the

Government nearly ruined the artist of the magnificent gates of the arch. Their cost was 3,000 guineas, and they are the largest and most superb in Europe, not excepting the stupendous gates of the Ducal Palace at Venice, and those made by order of Buonaparte for the Louvre at Paris. Yet the Government agents are reported to have conveyed these costly gates from the manufacturer's in a 'common stage wagon,' when the semi-circular head, the most beautiful portion of the design, was irretrievably mutilated; and, consequently, it has not been fixed in the archway to the present day."

At the same time, he wrote about some of the palace's more prominent features: "The most important portions of the palace are the Marble Hall and Sculpture Gallery, the Library, the Grand Staircase, the Vestibule, the state apartments, consisting of the New Drawing-room, and the Throne-room, the Picture Gallery (where her present Majesty has placed a valuable collection of paintings), the Grand Saloon, and the State Ballroom."

Members of the Royal Family with President Richard Nixon in the Marble Hall

Queen Elizabeth II with the First Couple in one of the private apartments in the north wing of the palace

The Queen's Gallery

According to Ruthven, the Entrance-hall was surrounded by double columns, each with gilded bases and capitals and all standing one base. He observed that each column consisted of one piece of Carrara marble and that the Grand Staircase, carved of white marble, was elaborately decorated. It, and much of the State Ballroom, was decorated by L. Gruner at a cost of around £300,000. Here, Victoria ordered hung the state portraits made of her and Albert by Winterhalter. They appeared during her reign alongside those of the doomed Charles I and his wife, Henrietta Maria.

The Library, which also served as a waiting-room for deputations, was "decorated in a manner combining comfort with elegance" and opened onto the terrace. From its windows one could see the chapel at one end and the conservatory at the other. But of course, the real beauty lay in its view of the gardens. Once those granted an audience with Her Majesty left this room, they passed through the Sculpture Gallery, where busts of important statesmen were housed, as well as those of members of the Royal Family, and into the Hall. Next, they proceeded up the Grand Staircase through another ante-room and into the Green Drawing Room, their last stop before the Throne Room itself. The Green Drawing Room opened onto the upper floor of the porch running along the old part of the building. It was, apparently, "a long and lofty apartment." Those not visiting the palace for an audience passed through the Green Drawing-room to the Picture Gallery or the Grand Saloon. Not surprisingly, the former housed some of the very finest pieces of art from the day and earlier, including works by Dutch and Flemish artists, as well as those of the Italian and English schools. The Picture Gallery itself was nearly 150 feet long and 150 feet wide and lighted by skylights which, while providing the area with excellent light, wreaked havoc on the paintings themselves.

The Throne Room, of course, was the most dreamed of destination, and it ran along the eastern side of the building for more than sixty feet. During Victoria's time, the walls were hung with crimson red satin and velvet, and the ceiling was richly carved and gilded. However, in Ruthven's mind, of all the more than 700 rooms in the palace, the Yellow Drawing Room was thought to be the most magnificent, for it featured elaborately carved furniture, much of which was overlaid with burnished gold and upholstered with broad-striped yellow satin. Located just outside the Queen's private apartments, its ceiling was supported by several polished marble pillars standing against the four walls, each of which featured a full-length portrait of a member of the Royal Family.

Near the Yellow Drawing Room lay the saloon, right at the center of the garden front. Ruthven described it as "superbly decorated," with purple scagliolan Corinthian columns carved to look like lapis lazuli. He insisted that "the entablature, cornice, and ceiling are profusely enriched; and the remaining decorations and furniture are of corresponding magnificence." Meanwhile, the South Drawing Room featured "compositions in relief," including those of Spenser,

Shakespeare, and Milton.

For the vast majority of people who will never see the inside of Buckingham Palace, the State Dining Room holds perhaps that most appeal, with its long table and rows of gilded chairs. Ruthven himself considered it "a very spacious and handsome apartment," pointing to the long row of windows that ran alongside and overlooked the garden. Between each window hung a long mirror designed to increase the light in the room. The ceiling was carved with "foliage and floral ornamentation" and portraits of deceased royals ran the length of the other side of the room.

The gardens at Buckingham Palace were never going to rival those at Kensington, but, as Horace Walpole observed, "The garden, or west front, of the palace, architecturally the principal one, has five Corinthian towers, and also a balustraded terrace, on the upper portion of which are statues, trophies, and bas-reliefs, by Flaxman and other distinguished sculptors. The pleasure grounds cover a space of about forty acres, five of which are occupied by a lake. Upon the summit of a lofty artificial mound, rising from the margin of the lake, is a picturesque pavilion, or garden-house, with a minaret roof. In the center is an octagonal room…"

On the north side of the garden lay the Royal Mews, or stables. There, each of Victoria's nine children took riding lessons, and there also were housed her more than 40 carriages, including the still famous State Coach designed by Sir William Chambers in 1762 and painted by Cipriani.

In 1851, Queen Victoria, or more precisely, her children, made history and set a new precedent when they became the first members of the Royal Family to appear on the balcony of Buckingham Palace during a public celebration. As Queen Victoria and Prince Albert left in procession to open the Great Exhibition, "a groundbreaking showcase of international manufacturing, masterminded by Prince Albert," the *London Daily News* reported, "At this moment the new front of the palace was put to a use never contemplated by those who have been so eager in their enunciation of the architect. The many windows gave to her Majesty's household the opportunity they never before enjoyed so perfectly of catalogue: seeing a state procession. The balcony over the center bronzed gateway was occupied by a most interesting party—the younger children of the royal the royal family, attended by several ladies."

The older members of the Royal Family appeared again on the balcony on March 1, 1854. The *London Express* reported, "The first battalion of the Scot Fusilier Guards paraded in front of Buckingham Palace at 7 o'clock yesterday morning, immediately after leaving the Wellington Barracks en route to Portsmouth, for embarkation on foreign service. Her Majesty, Prince Albert, the Prince of Wales, Prince Alfred, and the Princesses appeared on the balcony of the center window. The battalion, under the command of Colonel Dixon, being formed in line, presented arms, and gave three cheers, after which they marched to the Waterloo station on the South Western Railway."

The observation had been accurately made that Buckingham Palace is like a duck, sailing serenely across the water while its feet paddle frantically beneath the surface. While they are not typically frantic, those paddling beneath the surface in Victoria's day included hundreds of servants, led by the "Board of Green Cloth," a five member leadership team made up of the Lord Steward, the Treasurer, the Comptroller, the Master of the Household, and the Secretary. Together these five supervised the many separate departments of the royal household. According to Murray, writing in his *Official Handbook of Church and State*, "The Lord Steward of the Household...is the chief officer of the Queen's Household, all the officers and servants of which are under his control, except those belonging to the Chapel, the Chamber, and the Stable. His authority extends over the offices of Treasurer, Comptroller, and Master of the Household. The Lord Steward is at the head of the Court of the Queen's Household—the Board of Green Cloth. He is always sworn a member of the Privy Council. He has precedence before all peers of his own degree. He has no formal grant of his office, but receives his charge immediately from the Queen by the delivery of his white staff of office...He holds his appointment during pleasure, and his tenure depends upon the political party of which he is a member. ... The Lord Steward has the selection and appointment of all the subordinate officers and servants of the Household, and also of the Queen's tradesmen, except those connected with the royal stables...The Treasurer of the Household acts for the Lord Steward in his absence. ... The Comptroller is subordinate to the two preceding officers, for whom he acts in their absence. ... His particular duty consists in the examination and check of the Household expenses. ... The Master of the Household stands next in rank to this department. He is an officer under the Treasurer, and examines a portion of the accounts; but his duties consist more especially in superintending the selection, qualification, and conduct of the Household servants."

Modern History

Many royal households have been the sites of births and deaths, illnesses and recoveries, but only Buckingham Palace has hosted not one but two major operations performed upon a sitting monarch. The first took place on June 21, 1902, on the recently crowned Edward VII. The first word that there was trouble came that afternoon, when the palace announced simply, "King Edward is suffering from perityphlitis [appendicitis] and is undergoing a surgical operation." Then, on the 24th, the people were informed, "The operation has been successfully performed. A large abscess has been evacuated The king has borne the operation well and is in a satisfactory condition."

Encouraging bulletins continued to be posted, and the *Associated Press* eventually reported, "The King's doctors believe that his majesty would have been dead before now except for the operation. His condition became so alarming last night that at one time it was feared death might ensue before the surgeon's knife could afford him relief. Intense swelling of the-extremities, accompanied by alarming symptoms of mortification, constituted the emergency which demanded an immediate operation. To the last the king tried to avoid this, and he was willing to be carried to the abbey for the coronation ceremony, in order that it should occur as arranged...The influence of Queen Alexandra was enlisted, however, and at an early hour this morning the royal patient was prepared for the operation, which, even in the skillful hands of England's best surgeons, was fraught with grave danger. Shortly before 2 o'clock this afternoon his majesty was moved from his couch to the operating table and the anesthetic was administered. Sir Frederick Treves made the incision, near the patient's groin and carried it upwards, with an outward slant, for nearly four inches. The obstruction was removed and a tubing was placed in the affected intestine."

The second operation, performed in September 1951, was less successful, even though it occurred after medical science had advanced by nearly 50 years. King George VI was operated on in the hope that removing his lung might stop the spread of the cancer that had recently been diagnosed. The *Associated Press* reported on September 24, "The brief announcement said 'The king has had a restful night. His majesty's condition this morning continues to be as satisfactory aa can be expected.' It came after a Buckingham Palace source had reported that the king 'made it safely' through the first crucial night after his operation yesterday morning, Anxious Britons, who had prayed for the safety of their beloved monarch, got no indication of the king's exact condition in his battle the after effects of the surgery. ... Handwritten with soft lead pencil the bulletin was posted on a board attached to the fence in front of Buckingham Palace."

King George VI

In sickness and in health, the peopled gathered at the palace gates. The article continued, "A tall police inspector read the bulletin aloud over the heads of the jostling throng. People then lined up and filed slowly past for a firsthand look. … Medical authorities are in general agreement that the first four or five days after the operation are the crucial period. As the sovereign fought his lonely battle for life, a little group of Britons kept a prayerful vigil outside the gates of massive Buckingham Palace…They were joined after daybreak by persons on their way to work who stopped to ask "How is he," very much like old friends asking after a neighbor. Others, set for a longer wait in hopes of new medical bulletins on the king's condition, parked their cars in the mall near the palace or sat quietly around the nearby monument to Queen Victoria."

The public would only learn the exact nature of the king's surgery after his death a few months later in February 1952.

For all the many people throughout the centuries who have admired and held the Royal Family in the highest esteem, not everyone who has gathered in front of Buckingham Palace did so to see them or wish them well. For instance, in 1914, 20,000 women marched there to demand the right to vote in local and parliamentary elections. The press was not particularly impressed, as the *Telegraph* made clear when it told readers that the incident was a "serious fracas between the wild women and the police, in which the militants delivered a brief but furious attack on the constables." The article added that Emmeline Pankhurst, the leader of the group, "was able to offer little or no resistance, but shouting out that she had got to the palace gates, she was carried bodily by a chief inspector to a private motor which the police had in waiting."

Pankhurst

The protest made news around the world, with the *Associated Press* reporting, "While leading an army of women upon Buckingham palace. Mrs. Emmeline Pankhurst, leader of the militant suffragettes, was arrested. Immediately after King George and Queen Mary arrived from

Aldershot, where they have been for five days inspecting the great military establishment, the women gathered at Whitehall and moved toward Buckingham palace. ... Their majesties, however, had stolen a march upon the suffragettes, for, instead of going direct to Buckingham palace, upon their arrival they went to Marlborough house, the residence of Dowager Queen Alexandra...More than 2,000 policemen, detectives and soldiers were on duty in the streets and around the palace to prevent rioting. Home Secretary McKenna had sent word to the leaders of the women that King George would not receive them under any circumstances. but this did not deter them "If he won't see us we will see him," was the reply sent back to the home secretary. ... As Mrs. Pankhurst was being taken to Holloway jail she lost all control of herself. With blazing eyes she struggled in the grasp of the police men. meanwhile shrieking, "That's right; arrest me at the gates of the king. Go tell the king you have arrested me."

The women's demands were largely overshadowed by the economic condition in England, a situation that continued to be a problem in the early days of World War I. In September 1914, *The Times* reported that "the beginning of extensive interior decoration work at the palace has been hastened by the Queen's desire ... to give employment to a class of workmen who will be the first to feel the pinch of retrenchment owing to the war. Alterations include a large quantity of parquet flooring specially made by Messrs. Howard of Berners St., a class of work hitherto much in the hands of German makers."

Much of the work done at this time was on the queen's private apartments and Charles Allom, director of White Allom, praised her taste, especially the way in which she designed her bedroom. In *Decorative artists to the King and Queen*, he wrote, "The room has been structurally altered by throwing the private service corridor into it, and this has led to the occurrence of an unusual feature. The fireplace is left in the centre of the wall, (the openings in which are supported by columns) which was pierced to open up the corridor now utilized for a long range of wardrobes." He further praised the "soft color that enables it to blend charmingly with the furniture and many cabinets, which contain hundreds of small objets d'art, interesting souvenirs and mementos of many journeys and visits. Collections and purchases of works, representing all phases of the industrial arts in which Her Majesty takes so great an interest are here assembled, yet the coloring of the room, with its curtains of blue silk like the walls and a carpet of soft brown bordered with camel color on which is a pale blue rose and green design, brings the floor into harmony with the walls and furniture."

Sadly, as the war continued, there was less time and attention available for fixing up the palace. In fact, the building itself came under attack in October 1915, as Queen Mary noted in her diary: "[A]t 9.30 p.m. they were still sitting in the Palace in G.'s room when we heard a distant report (presumably a bomb) so we went on to the balcony when the gun in Green Park began firing and searchlights were turned on ... We did not see the Zeppelin but Derek saw it quite plainly from his house in Buck. Gate. We then heard some bombs being dropped and were told later that some had fallen in the Strand and elsewhere, killing 8 people and injuring 34. All quiet by 10.15."

The east wing of Buckingham Palace in the 1910s

The palace was spared that time, but Buckingham Palace would have less luck a few decades later as the nation once again lurched towards war with Germany. During World War II, the young princesses, Elizabeth and Margaret, were determined to do their part for the war effort. Living at the time in Buckingham Palace, they led the way in founding a Girl Guide Troop that met in the palace each week. Their aunt, Princess Mary, agreed to sponsor the troop and act as its leader.

The 1st Buckingham Palace Company counted among its members 20 Guides, including Princess Elizabeth, and 14 Brownies, including Princess Margaret. The other members were made up of other daughters of the royal household and even members of the palace staff. The king and queen gave the girls the use of a summerhouse for the headquarters, and in the years that followed, the young ladies were often seen pitching tents and cooking over open fires in the palace's extensive gardens. One press report told readers, "At present, the chief hobby of Elizabeth and Margarget, too, is Girl Guides. Both recently passed the tenderfoot tests and early this month their aunt, the Princess Royal, as president of the Girl Guides, will enroll them as 'guide' and 'brownie' respectively. With a group of young friends, children of neighbors when they lived in Piccadilly, they formed the 'First Buckingham Palace Company.' She is studying hard to pass the tests for patrol leader."

Elizabeth during the war

In the end, the girls lost their summerhouse at the beginning of World War II and had to move their activities to the more rural grounds of Windsor Castle. In fact, Buckingham Palace remained a German target throughout the war and was bombed on several occasions, particularly during the Battle of Britain. On September 11, 1940, the king wrote to his mother, "You will have heard about the time bomb which fell near the Garden Entrance at Buckingham Palace last Sunday night, & which exploded on Monday night. I am sending you photographs taken on Monday & Tuesday before & after the explosion showing the damage done…Except for damaging the swimming pool, the main structure of the Palace is untouched. All the windows on each floor were broken. The blast was all upward & only one ceiling is damaged. We were down here at Windsor luckily, & no one in B.P. felt the worse for the 'thud' as the bomb fell on Sunday night, though all our shelters are on that side. Everybody was evacuated on Monday night to the other side of the Palace, in case it exploded & it did at 1.25 a.m."

The official report read in part, "Time bomb has smashed many windows. Some of the ceiling in the Queen's small Chinese room is down. Some damage in Empire Room. The Queen's bedroom and boudoir comparatively undamaged apart from windows. Glass skylight over Minister's staircase is down. Swimming pool extensively damaged at end. Crater 15 ft wide where explosion occurred. No-one hurt. Great quantities of broken glass everywhere on that side of the Palace."

Another attack came days later on September 19, and the queen wrote to her mother-in-law about that one, which would end up being the worst attack the palace sustained: "[W]e heard the unmistakable whirr-whirr of a German plane…there was the noise of aircraft diving at great speed, and then the scream of a bomb. It all happened so quickly that we had only time to look foolishly at each other when the scream hurtled past us and exploded with a tremendous crash in the quadrangle…I saw a great column of smoke & earth thrown up into the air, and then we all dashed like lightening into the corridor. There was another tremendous explosion, and we & our 2 pages…remained for a moment or two in the corridor away from the stair case, in case of flying glass…[Men] were working below the Chapel, and how they survived I don't know. Their whole work-shop was a shambles, for the bomb had gone bang through the floor above them. … I went along to the kitchen which…has a glass roof. I found the chef bustling about…. He was perfectly unmoved…."

In his record of the incident, the king described it as "a ghastly experience yesterday & it was so very unexpected coming as it did out of low clouds & pouring rain at the time. We had just arrived at B.P. from here, & were still in our rooms upstairs. Elizabeth, Alec Hardinge & I were talking in my little room overlooking the quadrangle when it happened. We heard the aircraft, saw the 2 bombs, & then came the resounding crashes in the courtyard. Our windows were open, & nothing in the room moved. We were out of that room & into the passage at once, but we felt none the worse & thanked God that we were still alive…The door opposite the King's Door did not come down. All the windows windows were broken in the passage & the 2 full length pictures of the Duke & Duchess of Cambridge were perforated. But none of the others of the procession. The aircraft was seen flying along the Mall before dropping the bombs. The 2 delay action bombs in front of the Palace have exploded & part of the railings & centre gates are damaged…There is no damage to the Palace itself I am glad to say & no windows are broken. What a good thing it is that the Palace is so thin though & that the bombs fell in the open spaces. It was most certainly a direct attack on B.P. to demolish it, & it won't make me like Hitler any better for it."

The king and queen soon faced an awkward situation in figuring out how to entertain dignitaries in a severely damaged palace. In 1942, First Lady Eleanor Roosevelt visited England on a goodwill mission, and to help coordinate America's support for the British people. Queen Mary wrote to her mother, "It is so dreary at Buckingham Palace, so dirty & dark and draughty, & I long to see the old house tidy & clean once again, with carpets & curtains & no beastly air raids. I feel so sorry for poor Mrs. Ferguson & the housemaids, for it is most depressing having to look after a house that is half ruined! I am putting Mrs. R in my own bedroom upstairs. I have had some small windows put in, and she can use Bertie's own sitting room as mine is dismantled & windowless. It is quite a problem to put up one guest nowadays! She is only bringing a Secretary with her, & travels very simply & quietly."

The queen need not have worried, for though Mrs. Roosevelt had lived her entire life in wealth and privilege, she had still never experienced anything like Buckingham Palace, even in its damaged state. She recalled, "I had been a bit taken aback when I arrived at Buckingham Palace on that trip and was shown my dressing-room with huge closets all around the walls. The maid who unpacked my luggage was well trained but I could see that she was surprised when all she could find to hang up in the enormous expanse of wardrobes was one evening dress, one afternoon dress, a few blouses and an extra skirt!"

Even after the war was over, it still took years for the palace to be restored to its pre-war glory. The young princesses' governess, affectionately called "Crawfie," later wrote, "On wet days when we could not get out, Margaret would say, 'Let's explore.' Then we would wander off round the Palace, to the war-scarred and shut-off apartments where the workmen were busy. During the war the glass chandeliers had all been removed for safety, the pictures and ornaments packed away. Now they were back, waiting to be unpacked and returned to their places, and sometimes we took a hand. It was fun undoing the beautiful crystal pieces and china figures. There was no saying what we might find next. We polished with our handkerchiefs the bits we unpacked...And one day, pottering through the half-dismantled rooms, we came upon a very old piano. Margaret was delighted with this find. She dragged up a packing-case, sat down and proceeded to play Chopin. As she touched the notes, great clouds of dust flew out."

One of the biggest questions was what to do with the chapel that Queen Victoria put in after it had been bombed beyond repair. Finally, the decision was made to rebuild the "exterior without alteration, removing Pennethorne's defacements and restoring the original work of Nash. Pennethorne introduced height by raising the roof but instead of doing this the nave floor has been lowered so as not to interfere with the roof line as originally designed."

The work proceeded according to plan, but there was much more to be concerned about than simply a Victorian chapel. In 1947, Parliament received a report with a cost estimate: "The special work now in hand at Buckingham Palace includes bomb damage repairs, excavation work for a new boiler house and mains in connection with the modernization of the heating system, and the improvement of the servants' quarters in the attics. There is also some work in connection with redecoration of certain rooms and the re-wiring of part of the State rooms. The total cost of this work is about £54,300, of which about half is on bomb damage repairs...The number of men employed is 178. I am satisfied that this work is necessary. The general program for modernizing engineering services in the Palace will be spread over many years, but the opportunity has been taken of the absence of the Royal Family in South Africa to carry out certain noisy and dirty work connected with the installation of new boilers which will be oil fired."

Fortunately, the recovery moved on, and by the time Princess Elizabeth returned to the palace in 1947 with her new husband, the building was looking much better. They only lived there a few months before moving to what they hoped would be their permanent home at Clarence House, but Elizabeth returned to Buckingham Palace as queen just a few years later after losing her father, King George VI, in February 1952. It was difficult for her and Prince Philip to give up the cozy home they had created at Clarence House and move into the drafty palace, in spite of the fact that the new queen had already lived much of her life there. However, as duty always came first for the royals, back to Buckingham Palace they went, with the young prince and princess with them.

In the years that followed, Buckingham Palace continued to see its fair share of births and deaths, marriages, and, new to the later 20th century, divorces. In 1967, Prince Edward, Queen Elizabeth's youngest child, became the last baby to be born in the palace, the modern royals preferring hospital births. It is hard, and somewhat inappropriate, to speculate over if and when Buckingham Palace will be the site of another death for the Royal Family, but there will always be marriages to celebrate in the future. In July 1981, Prince Charles and his bride, Diana, made history and set a new precedent by being the first royal couple to kiss on the balcony, and it is now a much adored tradition. Unfortunately, Charles later became the first heir to the throne to divorce, and then later remarry. Today, he and his wife, the Duchess of Cornwall, live on a country estate and not at Buckingham Palace.

The coming of the 21st century has seen that palace modified and updated to keep current with the latest in technology. Cables run through the ancient walls and satellite dishes are placed discreetly on the roof, with care being taken to do nothing that would diminish the grandeur of the storied residence. The palace remains a large bow that ties the past and the present together, as author Edna Healy so aptly put it: "In 1995, on the fiftieth anniversary of VE Day, the victory in Europe, once again thousands thronged the Mall to cheer The Queen, Prince Philip and the royal family as they made their traditional appearance. As wartime songs rang across the Park, there were many who remembered the courage of King George VI and Queen Elizabeth, who had braved the bombs with the people of London. Viewers caught the unforgettable moment when Queen Elizabeth The Queen Mother, then ninety-five, gave her characteristic wave as she sang with the crowds the wartime song Wish me luck as you wave me goodbye'."

Prince William and President Barack Obama in the 1844 Room in Buckingham Palace

Brendan and Ruth McCartney's aerial photo of Buckingham Palace in the 21st century

Kensington Palace

William & Mary

Kensington Palace is a wonderful example of the idea that "from little acorns great oaks grow," as it was never intended to be a palace but merely a house. Far from being a royal residence, Kensington was originally a simple country estate built in 1605 for Sir George Coppin, a minor member of the court of King James I. The two-story Jacobean mansion was located outside of London, on the edge of the small village of Kensington. Sir George Coppin purchased the land on which it was built during the late stages of the reign of Queen Elizabeth I, and subsequently built his home on the land. In 1619, he sold the house and property to Heneage Finch, 1st Earl of Nottingham. Finch's son later inherited the estate.

King James I

1ˢᵗ Earl of Nottingham

In 1689, William III took the throne of England, along with his wife, Queen Mary. They ruled together and were, by all accounts, very devoted to each other. At the time, however, the royal residences then available to them were located along the damp and foggy River Thames, and the king suffered from asthma and needed a drier climate. Thus, the royal couple went shopping and ended up purchasing Nottingham House from Daniel Finch, the 2ⁿᵈ Earl of Nottingham and the king's own Secretary of State, for £20,000. According to Thomas Faulkner's esteemed *History and Antiquities of Kensington*, "It is difficult...to ascertain precisely, what part of the present pile of building was erected, previous to its being made a royal residence; but it is presumed, it must have been sufficiently capacious for a numerous household. It is probable the buildings surrounding the court yard on the west, which now forms the grand entrance, with the state apartments, usually shewn to strangers, and those now occupied by His Royal Highness the Duke of Sussex, in the south front, were parts of the original structure."

King William III

Queen Mary

2ⁿᵈ Earl of Nottingham

While the house was perfectly fine for a commoner or even a nobleman like the 2ⁿᵈ Earl of Nottingham, it was far from suitable for England's royal family, and William immediately sent for Sir Christopher Wren and commissioned him to expand and improve it. Faulkner explained, "That portion of the south front, which contains the King's gallery, and the apartments occupied by Her Royal Highness the Duchess of Kent, were built by King William, when Sir Christopher Wren, and Nicholas Hawksmoor, were the royal architects."

Wren

Hawksmoor

One can easily imagine that William III was not the easiest man in the world to work for, for he wanted the job completed both quickly and inexpensively. Fortunately, Wren was quite experienced at working with the aristocracy and was able to satisfy the king by building onto and around the existing house. He added a new three story wing to each side of the original mansion and moved the main entrance to the building to the west side, where he built the Great Court. He also put in the south wing the Stone Gallery, a long corridor leading from the Great Court to the rooms set aside for visiting courtiers. Opposite it were the kitchens in the north wing. Over this courtyard is an impressive archway and clock tower, which certainly served to remind the servants not to be late to work.

Steve Cadman's picture of the east front of Kensington Palace

A picture of the William III statue at the palace

The court moved to Kensington in 1689, and on February 25, 1690, diarist John Evelyn described it in writing: "I went to Kensington, which King William had bought of Lord Nottingham, and altered but was yet a patched building, but with the garden, however, it is a very sweet villa, having to it the Park and a straight new way through this Park."

By this time, William had moved on to a new project, namely defeating James II's attempt to usurp the throne, but in the meantime, Queen Mary decided to amuse herself by making some more additions to their home. She ordered the Queen's Gallery built, making her own apartments bigger and adding separate rooms to house her Maids of Honour.

19th century depictions of the Queen's Gallery

There was a near tragedy shortly thereafter. According to a 1691 report in the *London Gazette*, "Whitehall, November 11th. " Last night a fire happened in their Majesties palace at Kensington, which burnt down the stone gallery, but was happily stopped before it reached their Majesties apartments." Fortunately, Wren and his team were able to repair the damage and even improve the area, rebuilding the King's Staircase in marble and adding a Guard Chamber near its base.

19th century depictions of the Grand Staircase

Architects working on Kensington also built something else, as Lucy Worsley, Chief Curator of Historic Royal Palaces, noted: "The King's Grand Staircase at Kensington Palace was the official way up to the king's chambers, but there was also a small and secret service staircase elsewhere. This backstair was used by the servants and also by the king's favoured friends. Anyone hoping to sneak up the backstair would find one of the king's pages keeping guard. These gatekeepers wielded enormous influence, all the more so since Charles II (r. 1660-85) had delegated much control to one particular page, William Chiffinch (c. 1602-91)."

Like most royal residences, Kensington was far from homey, but many people, including children, did live and visit there, as the following story, told in the late 18th century by Lord Sackville demonstrates: "My father, having lost his own mother when very young, was brought up chiefly by the Dowager Countess of Northampton, his grandmother, who being particularly acceptable to Queen Mary, she commanded the countess always to bring her little grandson, Lord Buckhurst, to Kensington Palace, though at that time hardly four years of age; and he was allowed to amuse himself with a child's cart in the gallery…It happened that her Majesty having one afternoon…made tea, and waiting for the king's arrival…the boy, hearing the queen express her impatience at the delay, ran away to the closet, dragging after him the cart. When he arrived at the door, he knocked, and the king asked, 'Who is there?' 'Lord Buck,' answered he. 'And what does Lord Buck want with me?' replied his Majesty. 'You must come to tea directly,' said he; 'the queen is waiting for you.' ... King William immediately laid down his pen, and opened the door; then taking the child in his arms, placed Lord Buckhurst in the cart, and seizing the pole, drew them both along the gallery, quite to the room in which were seated the queen, Lady Northampton, and the company. ... The Countess of Northampton...would have punished him; but the king interposed in his behalf..."

This incident obviously happened sometime before Queen Mary's 1694 death from smallpox at the age of 32. The king, devastated by her loss, removed many reminders of their happy life together, including furniture she had purchased and her large collection of fine china. The following year, he brought Hawksmoor in to make an addition that became known as the South Front. It featured a long first-floor gallery, known as the King's Gallery, where William chose to hang his extensive collection of artwork.

Six years later, Evelyn made another note, this time observing, "I went to see the King's House at Kensington. It is very noble but not great. The gallery furnished with the best pictures [from] all the houses, of Titian, Raphael, Correggio, Holbein, Julio Romano, Bassam, Vandyke, Tintoret and others; a great collection of Porcelain; and a pretty private library. The gardens about it very delicious."

Writing in 1908, Lena Milman observed, "The doorways have charm, but it is of that intimate kind little adapted to palaces, and indeed Kensington is no palace except in name. ... The public entrance is now at the north-east corner by two doors, of which that in the east wall is very charming with the royal cipher carved above the door and a brick niche above. The Queen's staircase which leads to the state rooms is a masterpiece of homely, well-proportioned designing, its wall entirely wainscotted and its banister also of oak...Queen Mary's gallery, with its two fireplaces, deep window-seats, and modillion-borne cornice, has undergone no structural alteration, and retains its panelling. So does Queen Anne's dining-room, the cornice of which should be compared with that of Queen Mary's gallery. Queen Caroline's drawing-room was much injured by Kent, but its window commands a fine view of the Clock Court, of which the south and east sides are indubitably of Wren's building...The sunny King's gallery retains its original doorways, but its wainscot has gone, and a flat, gaudily painted false ceiling has been inserted in place of the plain ceiling gently arching from behind the cornice which formerly roofed this room in the same manner as the rest of the Wren-designed suite. ... The King's grand staircase, for all Kent's tampering, is for the most part of Wren's construction. The iron banister with oaken hand-rail, the low black marble treads of the stair, the black and white paving of the hall and landings -- in a these we discern Wren's taste."

The 18th Century

William outlived his beloved queen by only a few years, and when he died on March 8, 1702, Mary's sister Anne succeeded him. Anne was known for being dour, and for good reason; by the time she came to the throne, she had experienced 17 pregnancies in about as many years, most of which ended in miscarriage or stillbirth. Among the five children who were born alive, only three lived to see their second day of life, and only one past his second birthday. That son, her only heir, died at the age of 11, more than a year before Anne came to the throne. These losses took a huge physical and emotional toll on the queen, and by the time William died, she was suffering from depression and significant weight gain.

Queen Anne

Anne initially used Kensington more as a vacation home than a primary residence, but she did initiate a number of major additions. For one thing, she brought Wren in to finish the work he had done for William and Mary, being much less parsimonious than her predecessors. She designated these final additions the Queen's Apartments. They, in turn, were reached by the Queen's Entrance, which itself featured a specially designed, shallow staircase that the infirm queen could climb and descend with ease.

In spite of all this work, Anne's most significant change came during her early years as queen, a period in which she threw herself into improving the palace gardens. She brought Sir Wren back to design them and provided him with a sumptuous budget of more than £2,500. John Bowack, writing in 1705, gushed about the gardens: "There is a noble collection of foreign plants and fine neat greens, which makes it pleasant all the year, and the contrivance, variety, and disposition of the whole is extremely pleasing, and so frugal have they been of the room they had, that there was not an inch but what is well improved, the whole with the house not being above twenty-six acres. Her Majesty has been pleased lately to plant near thirty acres more towards the north, separated from the rest by a stately green-house, not yet finished ; upon this spot is near one hundred men daily at work, and so great is the progress they have made, that in less than nine months the whole is levelled, laid out, and planted, and when finished will be very fine. Her Majesty's gardener had the management of this."

The building in question was originally described as a greenhouse where expensive and exotic plants could be kept alive during the frigid English winters. It was also designed to shelter citrus trees, as its name indicates. However, as is so often the case with building projects, the structure soon grew much past its original plans and became something of a "summer supper house" where the king and queen could entertain, when the mood struck them.

Addison, writing for the *Spectator*, noted, "I shall take notice of that part in the upper garden, at Kensington, which was at first nothing but a gravel pit. It must have been a fine genius for gardening, that could have thought of forming such an unsightly hollow into so beautiful an area, and to have hit the eye with so uncommon and agreeable a scene as that which it is now wrought into."

Faulkner also described them in his 1820 work: "The superb building situated to the north of the palace, originally designed by Queen Anne for a banqueting house, and frequently used by her Majesty as such, is one story in height ; the south front consists of a centre, ornamented with four rusticated pillars, supporting a pediment, of the Doric order ; over which is a semicircular window ; both ends terminate in a semicircular recess; and the brickwork of the whole is justly admired. The interior is divided into three apartments, against the wall of the centre are placed pillars of the Corinthian order supporting a rich entablature The roofs of the circular pavilions at each end, are covered, and supported by eight fluted pillars of the same order."

Pictures of the palace's Sunken Garden

The work that Anne did on the palace was solely for her own comfort and that of her husband, Prince George of Denmark; she cared little for the comfort or even company of her courtiers. Sir John Clerk of Penicuik, who visited her shortly before Prince George died, observed, "No Court Attenders ever came near her. I never saw anybody attending there but some of her Guards in the outer Rooms, with one at most [or more?] of the Gentlemen of her Bedchamber. Her frequent fits of sickness, and the distance of the place from London, did not admit of what are commonly called Drawing-Room nights, so that I had many occasions to think that few Houses in England belonging to persons of Quality were kept in a more private way than the Queen's Royal Palace of Kensington."

Prince George of Denmark

As her health deteriorated, Anne enjoyed living at Kensington, primarily because it allowed her to see and be seen by only the people she chose to receive. The only time she ever left for any length of time was following the death of her husband in October 1708. He had died in his chambers at the palace, and she seemed to want to get away from unwanted memories. However, she returned there in 1710, and Kensington remained her primary residence until she died in 1714.

From the moment King George I came to the throne, he made it clear that he was a very different monarch than his predecessor, because while Anne had seen Kensington as something of a refuge, he considered it as a prime location for entertaining. The old queen was barely dead before he ordered a bonfire of celebration lit on the lawns and rolled out barrels of beer for his servants. These, along with more than 300 bottles of claret, led to some serious toasting and merrymaking. This was only the first of many such parties, and a special celebration was held on August 1 during each year of his reign.

King George I

When King George I visited Kensington, he was pleased with what he saw, but he was a king, not a building inspector, and he soon learned that, along with the crown and a palace, he had also inherited a number of problems from his predecessor. After hearing from various advisors about conditions at Kensington, he ordered a survey taken of the building in 1716, and the report was even more ominous than the rumors: multiple repairs needed to be made.

Naturally, the king determined that if he was going to have repairs made, he might as well go ahead and have some other improvements made, so he contacted Sir John Vanbrugh, one of the leading architects of the day, and asked him to draw up plans to expand and improve the building. King George I intended to make Kensington more like nearby Blenheim Palace, but Vanbrugh's plans, which may actually have dated back to before the king discovered the problems, proved to be too elaborate for George's taste and the nation's pocketbook. In the end, George gave the job to William Benson, who the king appointed to replace Sir Wren as Surveyor General in 1715.

Vanbrugh

In spite of his age, Sir Wren was not happy with being displaced, nor was his son, Christopher, who wrote, "April 26, 1715. -- Superseded: in the 86th year of his age and 49th of his surveyorship. ... And there arose a King who knew not Joseph [Acts vii.]. And Gallio cared for none of these things." Another contemporary of Sir Wren's, Ker of Kersland, noted, "It is very well known, that Mr. B. was a favourite of the Germans. So great that Sir Christopher Wren the famous Architect...was turned out of his employment of being Master of the King's Work, which he had possessed with great Reputation ever since the Restoration, to make way for this Favourite of Foreigners...Some time afterwards Mr. B. fell under the displeasure of the House of Lords who, therefore, in the year 1719, addressed His Majesty to remove and prosecute him and upon His Majesty's gracious answer to this Complaint he not only ordered the said Mr. B. to be removed from his employment but prosecuted according to law. Whereupon none doubted but this Gentleman was to be brought to justice accordingly."

Despite what was about to happen to him in the future, Benson began the work on the palace in 1718, executing his plan to tear down the original Nottingham House and replace it with three grand rooms, later known as the Privey Chamber, the Withdrawing Room and the Cupola Room.

When Benson fell into disrepute and his Deputy, Colen Campbell, was called upon to complete the work.

Worried more about style than substance, George insisted that the new rooms had to be painted in the most elaborate ways possible. Campbell contacted Sir James Thornhill, who was then the court's official painter, but Campbell wanted £800 just to do the Cupola Room, so the king instead hired William Kent, a relatively unknown painter who put in the much lower bid of £350. King George I had apparently seen some of his previous work and was quite enthusiastic about his skills, in spite of the fact that many others in the court were not such big fans of his work.

Kent

Kent seemed to believe that too much of a good thing was wonderful, so he began his work on the Cupola Room by painting the domed ceiling blue and gold. He then added a large panel painted with the Star of the Order of the Garter and painted the walls brown and gold. The room featured a number of marble niches in which he placed gilded statues in various poses.

While the king was pleased, Kent's fellow artists were not, and three of them, John Vandewart,

Jacob Rambour and Alexander Nesbot, reported on May 22, 1722, "We have been to Kensington and carefully viewed and considered the said painting, which we did find better than half done: But having examined the particulars thereof, we have observed, and 'tis our opinion, that the Perspective is not just; that the principal of the work, which consists in ornaments and architecture, is not done as such a place requires. Mr. Nesbot adds that the Boys, Masks, Mouldings, etc., far from being well, he has seen very few worse for such a place: and Mr. Rambour affirms that the said work, far from being done in the best manner, as mentioned in your letter, it is not so much as tolerably well performed. As for the quality of the Blew used in the work, Mr. Vandewart and Mr. Rambour declare that they can't judge whether it is true ultramarine, because it does not look fine enough, but Mr. Nesbot's opinion is that it is nothing but Prussian Blew, in which perhaps there may be some Ultra-marine mixt."

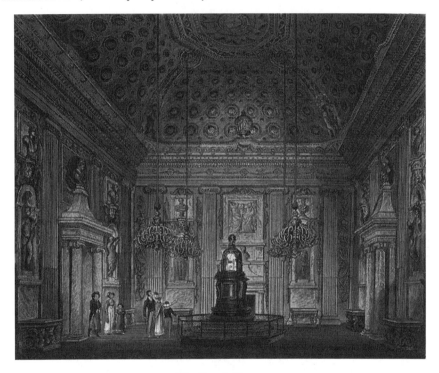

The Cupola Room

In spite of these criticisms (which had a noticeably xenophobic tinge related to the fact the Hanover line was German), George I stood by his man and commissioned Kent to decorate all the royal apartments at Kensington, a job that provided the artist with steady work for the next five years. His magnum opus proved to be the King's Grand Staircase, on which he painted portraits of 45 individuals then serving at court, including two Turkish men, some of the king's most personal servants. Worsley described its appearance at the time:

> "On the staircase Mohammed is boldly dressed in a blue cape, his eyebrow superciliously curved. His colleague Mustapha is older, white-bearded, turbaned. Mustapha presents a more exotic appearance and his waistcoat still bears a Turkish crescent moon over his heart.

> "When choosing his sitters for the stairs, William Kent was attracted to pretty faces. One of these belonged to Mrs Elizabeth Tempest, milliner to George I's daughter-in-law Caroline, Princess of Wales.

> "Kent also included a number of scarlet-clad Yeomen of the Guard.

> "A plainly-dressed gentleman in the north-east corner of the staircase has long been known as 'The Mysterious Quaker'.

> "The Wild Boy…was a feral child kept at court as a kind of pet. He had been discovered in 1725 all alone in the woods near Hanover eating acorns and William Kent depicts him with a sprig of oak in his right hand.

> Finally, on the ceiling above the staircase, William Kent added four more personal portraits. … He included a portrait of himself that expresses his extrovert character: plump, jolly and smiling. … Whispering into Kent's left ear is the lady presumed to be his lover, the formidable Elizabeth Butler."

The work King George I ordered done ensured that things were constantly frenetic at Kensington Palace, so much so that the king was rarely able to enjoy the fruits of the labor. However, on the rare occasions when he was there, he did make good use of his elaborately painted private apartments, preferring them to the more formal rooms set aside for state purposes. These were left for King George II, who succeeded him in 1727. Likewise, King George II spent much, but not all, of every year in the palace, becoming one of the last reigning monarchs to make it a primary residence. Thanks to his predecessor, Kensington was in tiptop condition when he moved in, so he did very little work on it during his lifetime.

King George II

The one building that King George II added was not to house people but horses; his younger son, William, was a tremendous riding enthusiast, so George ordered a stable built for him in 1740. For the most part, the king focused his attention - or more precisely, allowed his wife, Queen Caroline, to focus her attention - on updating and furnishing the interior of the palace. In 1729, she ordered "the delivery to the Honorable Grey Maynard, Yeoman of the King's removing wardrobe, the following for the King's service at Kensington, 16 pieces of crimson harrateen for furnishing the Prince of Wales's apartment with crimson silk lace, crimson harrateen furniture, with complete bedding for three press beds, crimson serge cases for three forms and six stools...." The order also listed "a curtain and valance of red taffeta, trimmed with red lace, for a closet joining to the Princess Royal's dressing-room. Also to give orders for putting handles and castors to the walnutted frames in the Queen's gallery, and to order the upholsters, joiners and cabinet makers to Windsor to remove furniture to be put up at Kensington…"

Queen Caroline

This is not to say that the queen had no interest in practical matters, as the Ranger of Hyde Park, which leads to Kensington, learned after receiving the following missive: "The King's ministers being very much incommoded by the dustiness of the road leading through Hyde Park now they are obliged to attend her Majesty at Kensington, the Lords of the Treasury have commanded me to acquaint your Lordship that it is her Majesty's pleasure that the said whole road be kept constantly watered instead of the ring in the said park, and that no coaches other than those of the nobility and gentry be suffered to go into or pass through the said park."

Queen Caroline, in fact, had more on her mind than just the dustiness of the road. She soon brought in Charles Bridgeman, a garden designer, who had succeeded Wise as royal gardener, to update the gardens around the palace. Preferring a more natural looking landscape, Bridgeman ordered the old-fashioned parterres removed and created the garden that is today world famous for its beauty and artistic layout. According to the London Parks and Garden Trust, "Queen Caroline annexed a further 300 acres from Hyde Park and set about its transformation, using Charles Bridgeman to produce a new design for the grounds. Bridgeman dug out a Round Pond and planted avenues of trees in front of the Palace, radiating out like the spokes on a wheel to give varied views of the Palace from different directions…Queen Caroline and Bridgeman arranged to have the Westbourne stream dammed to create a lake, the Long Water. Bridgeman came up with the idea of a ha-ha, or sunken ditch, to separate Kensington Gardens from Hyde Park. The gardens were open on Saturdays to the respectably dressed and it became fashionable for a while to stroll along the Main Path, the Broad Walk."

The lake in question, known as The Serpentine, was created by damming up the River Westbourne to combine its 11 natural ponds into one manmade lake. It was groundbreaking in its design - Bridgeman wanted it to look natural, as opposed to the traditional method of digging ponds in straight-sided lengths.

Thanks to all these efforts, and the thousands of pounds redecorating Kensington, the palace was one of the showplaces of Europe by the end of the 1730s, renowned especially for its paintings and fine furniture. However, following Queen Caroline's death in 1737, the king began to withdraw from the lavish entertainments he had previously thrown, and from caring for the comfort of the friends and relatives who stayed in the castle. In fact, he seems to have wanted to discourage anyone at all from visiting, as Horace Walpole, the Earl of Oxford, wrote to a friend in 1749: "Kensington Palace had like to have made an article the other night; it was on fire: my Lady Yarmouth has an ague, and is forced to keep a constant fire in her room against the damps. When my Lady Suffolk lived in that apartment, the floor produced a constant crop of mushrooms. Though there are so many vacant chambers, the King hoards all he can, and has locked up half the palace since the Queen's death: so he does at St. James's, and I believe would put the rooms out on interest, if he could get a closet a year for them!"

The 19th Century

On October 25, 1760, King George II became the last reigning monarch to die at Kensington Palace. His grandson and successor, King George III, preferred to live at Buckingham House with his ever-growing family. At first, he left Kensington largely empty, even opening the famed gardens to the public on Saturdays. In 1819, Faulkner observed, "the number of the gatekeepers have lately been increased, who are uniformly clothed in green. … The great South Walk, leading to the Palace, is crowded on Sunday mornings in the spring and summer with a display of all the beauty and fashion of the great metropolis, and affords a most gratifying spectacle, not to be equalled in Europe."

King George III

As each of his 15 children reached adulthood, the king had to find a place for them to set up their own households. While his older daughters married and move away, his older sons remained in London, often living lives of disrepute that embarrassed the royal family. Thus, in order to create some distance between himself and their often drama filled lives, he granted them apartments in other castles. In 1798, he gave his fourth son, Edward, the Duke of Kent, two floors in the south-eastern portion of Kensington Palace. Like his brothers, Edward was given these apartments with the understanding that he would settle down, give up at least his worst vices (in his case, gambling and mistresses), and find a wife.

Prince Edward

As the fourth son, it seemed unlikely that either Edward or his children would ever sit on the throne, so he was in no hurry to give up the pleasures of bachelorhood. And primary among these pleasures was decorating his new apartments to suit his taste. The rooms that Edward was assigned had been, in their prime, among the most luxurious in the palace, having been set aside for George II himself, but no one had lived in them since his death some 40 years earlier, so they were quite rundown. Edward begged and cajoled his father into financing some much needed renovations and commissioning James Wyatt, Surveyor-General to the Board of Works, to make massive changes to the first floor.

Wyatt

Wyatt soon learned that he had his work cut out for him, writing in 1810 "that the dry rot is making sad ravages in the Entrance Hall here," and claiming that it could easily spread to the upper floor. In addition to dealing with maintenance issues, Wyatt also designed a new porch to run along the east side of the Great Court. It featured a formal entryway that led to an elegant double staircase that in turn opened on to the Red Saloon. Here the Duke could entertain guests while waiting for dinner to be served in the nearby formal dining room.

In 1805, King George III sent his sixth son, Prince Augustus Frederick, Duke of Sussex, to live at Kensington, allotting him what would later be known as "Apartment I" in the southwest corner of the palace. Unlike his brother, Augustus was something of an intellectual, and he filled his apartments with fine art and scientific collections. He loved books and purchased more than he could ever read, creating a 50,000 volume library that filled 10 rooms at the palace. During his time as President of the Royal Society of London for Improving Natural Knowledge, he regularly entertained some of the leading scientists of the day, throwing lavish receptions marred only by occasional mishaps from the songbirds he allowed to fly about his apartments.

Prince Augustus Frederick

Prince Augustus Frederick, Prince Edward, and their brothers remained playboys for decades until November 1817, when Princess Charlotte, George III's only legitimate grandchild, died during childbirth. This left the family without a second generation heir and drove Edward and the others to look around for appropriate wives. Now 50 years old, Edward knew he would have a difficult time finding a wife among the youngest princesses in Europe, so he eventually married Princess Victoria of Saxe-Coburg-Saalfeld, a widow and Princess Charlotte's sister-in-law. They were married in Germany on May 29, 1818, and fortunately for the couple and the kingdom, Victoria was soon pregnant. As her due date drew near, Edward insisted that they return to England for the birth. Thus, in April 1819, the heavily pregnant princess made the difficult journey across Europe and the English Channel so that her child, a girl they named Alexandrina Victoria, could be born on May 24 at Kensington Palace. The child, who grew up to become the legendary Queen Victoria, would live at Kensington until ascending to the throne 18 years later. She later wrote, "My earliest recollections are connected with Kensington Palace, where I can remember crawling on a yellow carpet spread out for that purpose -- and being told that if I cried and was naughty my 'Uncle Sussex' would hear me and punish me, for which reason I always screamed when I saw him! ... I used to ride a donkey given me by my Uncle, the Duke of York, who was very kind to me. … To Tunbridge Wells we also went, living at a house called Mt. Pleasant, now an Hotel. Many pleasant days were spent here, and the return to Kensington in October or November was generally a day of tears."

Victoria as a teen

Victoria's mother, the Duchess of Kent

In explaining how she came to spend her childhood at Kensington instead of some other royal estate, Victoria noted that "George IV…had been on bad terms with my poor father when he died, -- and took hardly any notice of the poor widow and little fatherless girl, who were so poor at the time of his (the Duke of Kent's) death, that they could not have travelled back to Kensington Palace had it not been for the kind assistance of my dear Uncle, Prince Leopold."

Both George III and the Duke of Kent died before Victoria was a year old, leaving her to be raised by her mother, the Duchess of Kent. The Duchess soon found help in the conniving John Conroy. At this point, for little Victoria at least, Kensington Palace became more of a prison than a home. Biographer Kate Williams described these early years: "The duchess and Conroy attempted to bend Victoria to their will with a plan known as the 'Kensington system'. According to Victoria's half brother, Prince Charles of Leiningen, 'the basis of all actions, of the whole system followed at Kensington' was to ensure that the duchess had such influence over her daughter that 'the nation should have to assign her the regency', and the people would always associate her with Victoria. The aim was to make certain that 'nothing and no one should be able to tear the daughter away from her' … The Kensington system involved constant surveillance of the little girl 'down to the smallest and most insignificant detail'. Every cough, every piece of bread and butter consumed, every stamp of the tiny foot was reported to Conroy. The princess was forbidden the company of other children, and was never left alone. Although there were plenty of rooms, she slept in her mother's chamber and her governess sat with her until the duchess came to bed."

Part of the "Kensington System" included strengthening the Duchess of Kent's power by expanding the number of rooms she and the young Victoria occupied. Throughout the 1830s, she frequently fought with King William IV to gain more rooms than were already assigned to her, often claiming rooms for herself and her servants that had not been assigned to her by the king. She soon took over the State Apartments on the second floor, using them to entertain friends and hangers on in the hopes of solidifying her position at court.

In 1832, the Duchess brought in Sir Jeffrey Wyatville to divide what had been the King's Gallery into three smaller rooms. She said that they were for Victoria, who was now heiress presumptive. The Duchess also took over three rooms next to the gallery, which she had converted into a bedroom with an attached dressing room and a smaller room for her maid.

Of course, this kind of change could not stay secret long, and Charlie Greville later wrote of what happened next, a story he got from one of William's illegitimate sons. In 1826, the King "went to Kensington Palace to look about it; when he got there he found that the Duchess of Kent had appropriated to her own use a suite of apartments, seventeen in number for which she had applied last year, and which he had refused to let her have. This increased his ill-humor, already excessive. When he arrived at Windsor and went into the drawing-room…where the whole party was assembled…" Greville quoted the son as saying, "He then turned to the Duchess and made her a low box, almost immediately after which he said that 'a most unwarrantable liberty had been taken with one of his Palaces; that he had just come from Kensington, where he found apartments had been taken possession of not only without his consent, but contrary to his commands, and that he neither under stood nor would endure conduct so disrespectful of him."

In the end, neither the Duchess nor the king would win the "Battle for Kensington", for barely a year passed before William died and Victoria herself inherited the palace and control over all its rooms. However, she was anxious to leave it behind and move immediately to Buckingham Palace. Later, in 1843, when she had been married for a few years to her beloved Albert and was herself a mother, Victoria admitted, "I owe the present great domestic happiness I now enjoy, and which is much greater than I deserve, though certainly my Kensington life for the last six or seven years had been one of great misery and oppression, and I may expect some little retribution, and, indeed, after my accession, there was a great deal of worry."

Prince Albert

By 1855, it was becoming more common for commoners to be granted tours of Kensington, as John Timbs noted in *Curiosities of London,* "The great staircase, of black and white marble, and graceful ironwork (the walls painted by Kent with mythological subjects in chiaroscuro, and architectural and sculptural decoration), leads to the suite of twelve state apartments, some of which are hung with tapestry, and have painted ceilings. The 'Presence Chamber' has a chimney-piece richly sculptured by Gibbons, with flowers, fruits, and heads; the ceiling is diapered red, blue, and gold upon a white field, copied by Kent from Herculaneum; and the pier-glass is wreathed with flowers, by Jean Baptiste Monnoyer...The 'King's Gallery,' in the south front, has an elaborately painted allegorical ceiling, and a circular fresco of a Madonna, after Raphael. 'The Cube Room' is forty feet in height, and contains gilded statues and busts, and a marble bas-relief of a Roman marriage, by Rysbrack. The 'King's Great Drawing-room' was hung with the then new paper, in imitation of the old velvet flock...The 'Queen's Gallery,' in the rear of the eastern front, continued northwards, has above the doorway the monogram of William and Mary; and the pediment is enriched with fruits and flowers in high relief and wholly detached, probably carved by Gibbons. The 'Green Closet' was the private closet of William III., and contained his writing table and escritoire; and the 'Patchwork Closet' had its walls and chairs covered with tapestry worked by Queen Mary."

That same year, Leigh Hunt wrote, "It can be imagined full of English comfort, it is quiet, in a good air, and, though it is a palace, no tragical history is connected with it; all which considerations give it a sort of homely, fireside character, which seems to represent the domestic side of royalty itself, and thus renders an interesting service to what is not always so well recommended by cost and splendour. ...Kensington Palace seems a place to drink tea in; and this is by no means a state of things in which the idea of royalty comes least home to the good wishes of its subjects."

As time went on, Victoria continued the royal tradition set by her grandfather of giving rooms at Kensington to loyal courtiers. As a result, one more royal baby was born there, but not to a monarch. Among those given rooms by the queen over the years was Victoria's cousin, Princess Mary, Duchess of Teck, who lived there both before and after her marriage. In 1867, she gave birth to a daughter, Mary of Teck, who would herself become Queen of England some decades later following her marriage to the future George V. Mary of Teck was not only the last royal to be born at Kensington but the last English consort to be born royal.

Mary of Teck

In 1873, Victoria gave the famous Apartment 1 to her own daughter, Princess Louise, who had married in 1871. While George III might have used Kensington to keep his sons away, Victoria used it to keep Louise close, preventing her from having to make a home in Argyll. A bohemian, at least by Victorian standards, Louise was an accomplished artist, and she turned one of her rooms into an art studio. She also made another change to her apartments when she ordered her first floor windows bricked up after learning her young husband was going in and out of them during the night to visit his mistress. Except for their time serving in Canada, Louise lived at Kensington until her death in 1837.

If Victoria kept Louise close, she kept her younger sister, Beatrice, closer, insisting that she live with her wherever she was. However, after Beatrice's husband died, the queen came to see that this now middle-aged woman needed a home of her own and thus granted her the apartments in which she and her mother occupied when she was a child. They were immediately below Louise's rooms.

Unfortunately, when Beatrice moved in near the end of the 19th century, she found nothing about the rooms themselves that could comfort her, for they had by this time been used for decades as glorified storage space, holding artwork and furniture that were not wanted in other royal households. The building itself was also in need of repairs, with large sections of wood and brick needing maintenance or replacement. One article described the palace at this time as "empty, bare, dreary, and comfortless [with] nothing but bare walls and bare boards."

With the condition of the building growing worse each day, Parliament began to push to have it torn down. However, the queen made it clear that she would never support this, so Parliament was forced to find a different solution. In 1897, Parliament decided to repair the building, on the condition that it could also be opened to the public as a museum. On January 9, 1898, the big announcement finally came: "Her Majesty, in her desire to gratify the wishes of Her people, has directed that the State Rooms at Kensington Palace, in the central part of the building, which have been closed and unoccupied since 1760, together with Sir Christopher Wren's Banqueting Room, attached to the Palace, shall after careful restoration be opened to the public, during her pleasure; and the Government will forthwith submit to Parliament an estimate of the cost of restoration."

As few days later, on January 12, 1898, *The Times* reported, " More than once, it has been seriously proposed to pull the whole building down, and to deal otherwise with the land, and Her Majesty's subjects ought to be grateful to her for having strenuously resisted such an act of Vandalism, and for having declared that, while she lived, the palace in which she was born should not be destroyed."

When the work began, there was more to do than see. In January 1898, the *Westminster Budget* reported, "The very approach told of desertion and mystery. Grass grows between the cobblestones in the courtyard leading to the chief entrance; the tiny leaded window panes in the old brick walls look veiled and dolled with dust, and silence reigns supreme. You enter furtively and ascend by the grand staircase, the glory of the days of the early Georges. But its grand black marble is covered with boards; the graceful ironwork of its banisters is green with damp…The floors are up; you look into black abysses below the boards; the walls are bare, the grey day looks through cob-webbed windows upon a scene of utter desolation. … In the long picture galleries tall statues dressed in gilt paint and thick winter coats of dust stand together; the fireplaces are basins of red rust; the workmen are there, and a few visitors try to make their way about without falling into the holes in the floors…. The priceless pictures that once, adorned these walls, now covered with hideous cheap paper, the masterpieces of the Dutch, the Spanish, the Italian, and British artists…. Not a vestige remains, not even a mark against the wall where they have hung."

Once the word was out about the repairs planned, newspaper reporters began to swarm the palace, informing their readers of the hard times the former scenes of glory had fallen on. On January 28, 1898, *The Times* reported: "The exquisite interior has been the victim not merely of neglect, but of chronic outrage. For, as the little garden between this and the Palace has been found a convenient place on which to put up the glasshouses, frames and potting-sheds necessary for the park gardeners, what more natural, to the official eye, than that the Orangery close by should be pressed into the same service? Accordingly, at some time or other, which cannot have been very many years ago, more than half the beautiful high panelling of this building was torn down and has disappeared, the gardeners' stands have been let into the walls, and there the daily work has proceeded with no thought that it was daily desecration."

In 1899, Earnest Law observed in his guidebook for Kensington Palace, "It was found necessary to rebuild and underpin walls, to reslate practically the whole of the roof over the State Apartments and renew the timbers that carried it; and also almost all the floors. ... [Then the] business involved in the restoration of the old decorative ironwork, woodwork, and paintings of the State Rooms was taken in hand. ... Nor has any trouble, labour, or research been spared to render everything as historically and archeologically correct as possible…the most studied care has been taken never to renew any decoration where it was possible to preserve it — least of all ever to attempt to 'improve' old work into new. On the contrary, repairing, patching, mending, piecing, cleaning, have been the main occupations of the decorators, to an extent that would render some impatient, slapdash builders and surveyors frantic…Yet it has been all this minute— though no doubt sometimes costly — attention to details, this laborious piecing together of old fragments, this reverential saving of original material and work, this almost-sentimental imitation of the old style and taste where patching in by modern hands was inevitable, which has produced a result and effect likely, we think, to arouse the admira-tion of all who relish the inimitable charm of antique time-mellowed work."

Viscount Esher, who was the Secretary to the Office of Works, insisted that the house be restored "as far as possible [to] exactly what it was in the reign of George II."

Later that year, the *Kingston Gleaner* reported, "The apartments, which are shortly to be thrown open, are twelve in number, and are reached by way of the great staircase of black and white marble and graceful ironwork. Some of the State rooms are hung with tapestry, and have painted ceilings. The Presence chamber has a chimney-piece richly sculptured by the incomparable Grinling Gibbons with flowers, fruits and heads, a form of decorations wherein he excelled. The ceiling is diapered red, blue, and gold, upon a white field, copied from Heroulaneum by Kent, and the pier-glass ia wreathed with flowers, Jean Baptiste Monuoyer…The King's Gallery, in the south front, has an allegorical ceiling and a cicular fresco of a Madonna,. A lofty apartment, known aa the 'Cube Room,' is remarkable for its glided statues and busts as well as a baa relief in marble of a Roman marriage, by Rysbrack while the 'King's Great Bowing Room' overlooks the gardens towards the Round Pond. The 'Queen's Gallery,' situated at the rear of the eastern front, has above the doorway the monogram of William and Mary, and the pediment is in high relief and wholly detached —an example of carving which has been attributed to the wonderful Gibbons."

The official opening took place on May 24, 1899, in honor of the queen's 80th birthday. In spite of the overall plans laid out by Esher, not everything in the palace resembled the era of King George II. The *London Daily Mail* told readers, "The bedroom used by her Majesty as a child, which commands a superb view of the Round Pond, will contain show-cases full of the toys with which the young Princess beguiled the hours of play; and in an antechamber her doll's house will, no doubt, be of special interest to those who may desire to see how the fashion in these things has changed in seventy years…In the spacious King's Gallery, which locks full to the south, have been placed many fine paintings, mostly of naval scenes, by Wright, Sarres, and others. Here, as in the other state apartments, the furniture is of the Queen Anne period, and has, like the pictures, been brought from the various other royal palaces. The mantelpiece in the King's Gallery is a piece of superb carving in deal, which has been wonderfully toned down, while the centerpiece is a wind-dial of the period of Henry VIII."

In 1899, a contemporary guidebook announced, "The State Rooms of Kensington Palace, and likewise Queen Anne's Orangery, will be open to the public every day in the week throughout the year, except Wednesdays, unless notice be, at any time, given to the contrary. The hours of opening will be 10 o'clock in the morning on week days, and 2 o'clock in the afternoon on Sundays. The hours of closing will be 6 o'clock in the evening from the 1st of April to the 30th of September, both days inclusive, and 4 o'clock during the winter months. They will be closed on Christmas Day and Good Friday."

Peter Symonds' picture of the Queen Victoria statue at Kensington Palace

The Modern Era

The public embraced the opened palace from the very beginning but those in charge felt that it could be used for more than just showcasing Queen Victoria's toys or King George II's bed. Thus, in 1912, the State Apartments were given to the London Museum to be used to house and display interesting items from the City of London, as well as other possessions belonging to former monarchs. On March 25, 1911, the *London Standard* reported, "The proposed London Museum is now to enter the region of actualities…It must, of course, eventually obtain a local habitation of its own, a building not unworthy, we may hope, of its contents. In the meanwhile the King has temporarily placed the state apartments of Kensington Palace at the disposal of the trustees, and in these fine rooms the collection will presently be displayed for the edification and instruction of the citizens of London and those who visit their city…The museum is intended to perform for London the functions of the Musée Carnavalet in Paris. It is to illustrate the archaeology, sociology, domestic economy, art work, industrial, military, commercial, and ecclesiastical activity of London throughout the whole period of its long and chequered history. … Materials there are already in abundance, and more will be accumulated."

The museum was a pet project of Queen Mary's, and she was the one who persuaded the king that her birthplace could be put to good use in this way. In fact, she and King George V toured the museum on March 21, 1912. According to the *London Standard*, "Accompanying the King and Queen were Princess Mary and Prince George, and on reaching the museum their Majesties were received by Mr. Harcourt; Viscount Esher, and Earl Beauchamp, the three trustees, and also by Mr. Guy Laking, the curator of the museum. ... Their Majesties were conducted to the galleries, where they were met by Princess Henry of Battenberg, Princess Louis of Battenberg and her children, and the Duke of Teck. ... Mr. Guy Laking conducted the King, who constantly asked interesting questions, while Viscount Esher conducted the Queen. The other members of the royal family accompanied them in the inspection...In the first gallery his Majesty, as a keen sportsman, took special interest in pictures of tiger hunting in India by the late King and others, and stopped to examine closely a rhinoceros skull discovered in Fleet-street. In a bronze statue of the Emperor Hadrian his Majesty recognized a cast of the bronze statue in the British Museum."

King George V

Then there was this amusing anecdote: "Standing before the case containing the Coronation robes of King Edward and Queen Alexandra, the King asked if his mother approved of the display of jewels on the neck and breast of the lay figure used for displaying the dress, and was informed that her Majesty specially desired that the jewels should be displayed. The diamond collar and manifold string of pearls are, of course, clever imitations. The King agreed that the jewels certainly set off the dress and made the exhibit more effective."

In many ways, World War I turned Europe on its head, and so it was with Kensington Palace. With war clouds gathering, its museum collections were moved to Lancaster House in London's West End, and during the war, the king turned Kensington over to a number of war-time organizations to house their London offices.

Unlike many homes owned by the English nobility, the palace could not be used as a hospital for one simple reason: it was not fit for it. Toward the end of the war, the *Oshkosh Daily Northwestern* explained that "Buckingham, Kensington and St. James' palaces cannot be used as hospitals until their drainage system has been modernized. The palaces are relics of unenlightened, unregenerate days."

The crown issued the following statement in 1917: "In August, 1914, Kensington palace and St. James' palace were offered by the king to the Red Cross; but both these buildings were found to be unsuitable for the purpose of a hospital for several reasons, notably the absence of an efficient drainage system…It having been reported that there was no existing further demand for beds for the wounded in London, the king came to the conclusion that an expense of creating an efficient drainage system, putting in elevators, building a separate entrance could hardly be justified, and that it would be wiser for him to give a large subscription to the general committee of the Red Cross and Order of St. John of Jerusalem than to spend money in these directions…Kensington palace has been handed over to Lady Maedonnell for the Irish regiments' comforts fund. The question as to whether any of the apartments at present occupied by associations supplying comforts to the troops, or even the state apartments at Buckingham palace could be profitably used for government purposes, is still under consideration by the commissioner of public works."

In addition to those working in the palace, there were still a number of royals living in the palace, including Helena, the Duchess of Albany (the widow of Queen Victoria's son, Prince Leopold). Her daughter, Alice, was married to Alexander Cambridge, whose sister was Queen Mary. They also lived at Kensington, and Princess Victoria of Hesse moved there after she lost her husband. As more and more monarchs were displaced and came home to Kensington, Edward VIII coined the term "aunt heap" for the palace.

By this time, Queen Mary had set aside three rooms in the southeast corner of Kensington and restored them to the way they had looked when Queen Victoria had lived there as a girl. The news services reported, "Queen Victoria's rooms in Kensington Palace have been reopened to the public, restored to practically the same condition as they were a century ago when Queen Victoria occupied them with her mother, Duchess of Kent. Queen Mary, who was born at Kensington Palace, has taken the greatest interest in the scheme for refurnishing and decorating the rooms. She has made a careful inspection to see no detail has been overlooked…A large number of articles of furniture associated with Queen Victoria have been brought to the apartments from Frogmore. Visitors now see the royal apartments as they were in Queen Victoria's day—the sofa-table, the quaint chiffonier, the tapestry and chintz of the Victorian period, all are there, as well as many of Queen Victoria's toys. The apartments look out toward the famous Round Pond in Kensington Gardens."

Inevitably, Kensington Palace's fame and popularity, not to mention its location, made it a prime target for Nazi air raids during the Battle of Britain in 1940 and 1941. The *Canadian Press* reported at the time, "The Governor-General and Princess Alice learned some time ago from a friend in London of the damage to Kensington Palace by incendiary bombs. It was said at Government House today. 'Damage was not nearly as much as might have been expected," said a Government House spokesman.' ... according to word received at Government House shortly after the bombing the Princess' bedroom suffered damage from water during fire-fighting operations. The bedroom of her daughter, Lady May Abel Smith, was more seriously damaged but the governor-general's bedroom escaped harm. No word was received of damage to furniture or other valuable furnishings. Best news was that nobody was hurt, the spokesman said, adding, 'It seems to have been a lucky escape.'"

The north side of the main courtyard was hit hardest, and the area traditionally known as the Queen's Apartments also suffered heavy damage, but not all the damage to the palace during World War II was done by the Germans. The headquarters of Personnel Section had its offices there, in Apartment 34, for the duration of the war, and as a result, there were anti-aircraft guns and sandbags all over the lawn, with soldiers regularly digging trenches into the manicured grass.

Repairs on the palace proceeded slowly following the war, as there were not the time and resources available to move quickly. Prince Philip stayed there, with his grandmother, in 1947, as he awaited his marriage to Princess Elizabeth. Two years later, in 1949, the royal family was finally able reopen the now repaired State Apartments, and in 1950, the London Museum returned to the property.

Elizabeth and Philip

In the years that followed, many of the older royals from Queen Victoria's era grew old and died, leaving the palace increasingly vacant and forgotten. During the 1950s, Kensington became somewhat synonymous with a bygone era, as those left in residence were, if not old, than at least highly conservative and set in their ways. The 10th Duke of Beaufort, Henry Somerset, lived there, as did the queen's private secretary.

Then, in 1955, the mood in the palace began to lighten as the fashionable and charming Princess Marina of Greece and Denmark, Duchess of Kent moved in with her children. She had lost her husband, the queen's Uncle George, during World War II, and she needed a home for her family. Queen Elizabeth II gave her part of Princess Louise's former apartment, creating Apartment 1A. As fate would have it, she lived there for only 13 years before dying of a brain tumor in 1968.

Princess Marina

By this time, a new generation of royals had moved into Kensington Palace. The Queen's jet-setting sister, Princess Margaret, settled into Apartment 10 with her new husband, Antony Armstrong-Jones. Margaret called the suite of rooms, formerly occupied by one of Queen Victoria's last living grandsons, "the doll house," and she soon set about renovating it. Just a few weeks after their wedding, reporter Stan Delaplane wrote, "There is a good deal of talk and interest about Princess Margaret and Antony Armstrong-Jones. As you know, the couple will set up housekeeping next month. The Queen will give them a grace-and-favor house. That is the royal way of saying, for free. Anyway, we all agreed that Antony is one-up without a mortgage problem. But we further state that the maintenance will be a killer. The couple will get Kensington Palace…The milkman for Kensington Palace is Mr. Fred Smith. He has shown a proper spirit. 'I am delighted with the news,' said Mr. Smith. 'I shall be pleased to serve the princess.' He did not mention Antony. But I don't think he will short him on the cream or anything. Smith has estimated the couple's needs. 'I should think they will have about 8 pints of milk a day and 12 dozen eggs a week.' He did not say how he arrived at this figure. But he serves the Duchess of Kent and Princess Alice. So we suppose he knows a royal appetite. That is a great deal of milk and eggs. Even without a mortgage to pay off, the household bills will be a fair tab…The way we worked it out on paper, Antony is not going to come out ahead on grace-and-favor. It looks good. But did you ever pay for a complete new plastering job? That's just ONE thing we foresee." In fact, Armstrong-Jones did not have to pay to have his new home renovated but this was not necessarily a good thing. As a royal residence, Kensington fell under the Department of the Environment and 1960s English citizens were not inclined to spend freely. The Department gave the Princess and her husband a strict budget of £85,000."

Eric Koch's picture of Princess Margaret

Unfortunately for the Department, Margaret was accustomed to having her own way, and before anyone could stop her, she brought in contractors to pull out every wall and floor on the three main stories. She and Snowden tapped Carl Toms, a theatre designer, to help create the look of their new home, and when the work on these rooms was complete, there was a new reception room and three large bedrooms, each with its own dressing room. There were three new bathrooms and a nursery, as well as rooms devoted to linens, glassware and luggage care. There were also accommodations for the palace's large support staff, including nine bedrooms, four bathrooms, two kitchens and two sitting rooms. Armstrong-Jones had his own dark room, and Margaret had room after room decorated in her favorite colors, royal blue and pink. The two moved into their renovated home on March 4, 1963.

For the next two decades, the glamorous Princess Margaret remained the most well-known inhabitant of Kensington Palace until 1981, when Prince Charles brought his beautiful young bride, Diana, to live there. Apartments 8 and 9 were combined for their use, and it remained their London home and the place where they raised their sons, William and Harry. In 1988, *People Magazine* described life at Kensington: "The walls of Kensington Palace offer the family privacy and, according to Andrew Morton, author of Inside Kensington Palace, it is a child's paradise, with endless hallways in which to run and vast gardens for playing hide-and-seek. Morton suggests that the family's favorite spot is their railed roof garden, featuring a greenhouse (boasting clematis and miniature tomatoes) and a barbecue where Charles likes to grill salmon steaks, corn-on-the-cob and potatoes in foil, while Di sunbathes and the boys play on their slide-and-swing set...The children's two-room nursery (one room for sleep, one for daytime play) is in the attic just above Charles and Di's bedroom. The boys have their own bathroom outfitted with child-size toilets and washbasin. Further along the corridor, nannies Ruth Wallace and Olga Powell have their own bed-sitting-room. Charles and Di, though early risers, writes Morton, awaken many a morning to the thump-thump-thump of vigorous play overhead...From their nursery windows (barred for safety) the boys can see the royal helicopter pad, a particular fascination for William, who imitates the ground crew's arm signals and knows the names of most of the Queen's pilots. One of his first words was 'plane.'"

Elke Wetzig's picture of Charles and Diana

Sadly, the relationships within the family were not nearly as idyllic as their physical surroundings, and when Charles and Diana separated in 1992, they took separate apartments in the palace but remained under the same roof until Diana died in 1997. Her death brought the palace into the public eye in a way it had never been before. Writing of their "Pilgrimage to

Kensington Palace," sociologists George Monger and Jennifer Chandler observed, "A great many images, messages and floral tributes were fixed to trees in the area in front of the palace. At the base of the trees were candles, joss sticks and other offerings (including a garden gnome). Objects were also hung in the branches of trees…as well as lanterns, candles and flowers. These 'tree-shrines' had scarcely begun on the Tuesday but by Friday were an important element of the scene. Trees are obviously a convenient place to lean or hang flowers or to ensure that the tribute and message could seen, but beyond that were intentionally given a shrine-like appearance…Similarly, 'ground shrines…' also developed: one such consisted of a small plastic effigy of the Virgin Mary, crowned, robed in white and holding a rosary with two votive candles and a basket of white roses with blue statice and white 'baby's breath.' Nearby was a green heart-shaped candle. The whole was surrounded by bunches of flowers. Similarly, a sandbucket next to the railings at Hyde Park (which were covered in flowers and written messages and tributes) was transformed into an altar with a photograph of Diana surrounded by flowers and candles like an icon…This quasi-religious parallel to the phenomenon at Kensington Palace brings back the concept of the visit and taking of an offering as a form of pilgrimage, a feeling which was reinforced by the sight of people having their photograph taken with some of the floral tributes--evidence that they were there."

Maxwell Hamilton's picture of the flowers left at the palace for Diana

Diana lay in state at Kensington until, on the morning of September 6, a ringing bell announced that it was time for her funeral cortege to depart for her final public duty. Following her death, no one was anxious to move into her rooms. In fact, after lying empty for 10 years, they were converted into offices.

For the modern royals, Kensington Palace seems to be something of an extended home town, a place to go during both life's happiest and saddest moments. For instance, it was at Kensington that the Queen had her final, private viewing of her sister Margaret's body. With surprising restraint, the *Western Mail* reported in February 2002, "It was a poignant and very private occasion at Kensington Palace, the Princess's former London home. Looking sombre, the Queen arrived alone to say a personal final farewell to her younger sister who died on Saturday at the age of 71. The Princess's coffin, draped in her personal standard, was later being moved from Kensington Palace to the Queen's Chapel, St James's Palace, where it will remain until Thursday…As the coffin was leaving the Princess's former apartment, the Queen's Piper, Pipe Major James Motherwell, walked ahead of the hearse, playing a traditional lament. … Members of the Royal Family who live at Kensington Palace - including Princess Margaret's son Lord Linley, the Duke and Duchess of Gloucester, the Duke of Kent, and Prince and Princess Michael of Kent - were due to be present to say farewell as the Princess's body left her home."

For all its sentimental value, Kensington Palace is also often controversial. For instance, in 2008, Parliament demanded that Prince and Princess Michael of Kent either move out of their state-provided home or begin to perform a larger share of royal duties. On October 6, *The Telegraph* reported, "Buckingham Palace has confirmed that the royal couple will be charged the full commercial rate from 2010 to remain at their five-bedroom, five-reception home. The move followed demands by MPs on the Commons public accounts committee that full rent should be paid for the property after it emerged that the Prince and Princess were paying a nominal amount. The Queen has been covering the £10,000-a-month cost for her cousin and his wife to live at the royal residence since 2002…In 2002 it was agreed that rent should be paid on the apartment occupied by Prince and Princess Michael of Kent, and the Queen agreed to pay this rent from her own funds for up to seven years. The rent is paid to the Grant-in-aid, provided by the Government for the maintenance of the Occupied Royal Palaces. It has now been agreed that, from 2010, Prince and Princess Michael of Kent will remain at their apartment but pay the rent from their own funds…The apartment will be the couple's main home after they sold their Gloucestershire country mansion of Nether Lypiatt, near Stroud, in 2006. The royal couple has been using the apartment since 1979 when the Queen made it available to them. Before 2002, the Prince and Princess had been paying only a peppercorn rent that covered their utility bills for the apartment."

Today, the very popular Duke and Duchess of Cambridge keep a set of rooms in Kensington for their family to use when in London. They live in Apartment 1A, once the home of the stylish Princess Margaret, and their space consists of 20 rooms located on four separate floors. To get the palace ready for the young couple, the government spent £4.5 million to update the palace's heating, plastering and electric system. Much of the large budget went to remove asbestos from the rooms and put a new roof on the palace.

The Duke and Duchess moved in to their newly renovated digs in 2013, just after the birth of their first child. They kept many of the building's original features but changed the paint to the type of softer tones that Kate prefers. Prince Harry also keeps a smaller apartment in the palace, so he is often nearby to help his young niece and nephew find the best places in the palace to play.

Online Resources

Other books about English history by Charles River Editors

Other books about Buckingham Palace on Amazon

Other books about Kensington Palace on Amazon

Bibliography

"Kensington". Chambers's Encyclopaedia. London. 1901.

Faulkner, Thomas. *History and Antiquities of Kensington*

Goring, O. G. (1937). *From Goring House to Buckingham Palace*. London: Ivor Nicholson & Watson.

Harris, John; de Bellaigue, Geoffrey; & Miller, Oliver (1968). *Buckingham Palace*. London: Nelson.

Healey, Edma (1997). *The Queen's House: A Social History of Buckingham Palace*. London: Penguin Group.

Impey, Edward. *Kensington Palace: The Official Illustrated History* (London, 2003).

Lysons, Daniel. "Kensington", Environs of London, 3: County of Middlesex, London: T. Cadell (1792)

Mackenzie, Compton (1953). *The Queen's House*. London: Hutchinson.

Nash, Roy (1980). *Buckingham Palace: The Place and the People*. London: Macdonald Futura.

Peacocke, M. D. (1951). *The Story of Buckingham Palace*. London: Odhams Press.

Robinson, John Martin (1999). *Buckingham Palace*. Published by The Royal Collection, St James's Palace, London

Wright, Patricia (1999). *The Strange History of Buckingham Palace*. Stroud, Gloucs.: Sutton Publishing Ltd.